Reading between
the lines

The UK's leading handwriting expert Emma Bache has worked as a graphologist since 1989, analyzing handwriting in both the corporate and private sectors. With additional qualifications in psychotherapy and hypnotherapy, Emma has helped to solve cases of fraud for both private individuals and the corporate world, giving valuable insight into the criminal mind. She has had her own columns in *The Times* and the *Financial Times* and has written for other major publications such as the *Daily Mail*, the *Daily Telegraph*, the *Guardian* and *Cosmopolitan*. She has made frequent television and radio appearances, including GMTV's *This Morning*, BBC's *History Hunt* and Radio 4's *Today* programme.

Reading between the lines

What your handwriting

says about you

EMMA BACHE

Quercus

First published in hardback in Great Britain in 2018 by
Quercus Editions Ltd

This paperback published in 2019 by

Quercus Editions Ltd
Carmelite House
50 Victoria Embankment
London EC4Y 0DZ

An Hachette UK company

ISBN 978 1 78747 056 9
Ebook ISBN 978 1 78747 057 6

Printed

CONTENTS

In loving memory of my father,
Bill Hutchinson.

INTRODUCTION

I was a curious and nosy child. In my spare time I would often rifle through my parents' cupboards and drawers, reading anything and everything I could get my small hands on: old shopping lists that had been scribbled in a hurry, exquisitely penned private letters, carefully transcribed official documents.

Over the years, I fell in love with the handwritten word – its sheer beauty and individuality, but in particular the way it reveals the key to the writer's personality. I knew there was so much more to a scrawled message than just the words on the piece of paper. I found myself an inspirational tutor and took classes at the Roehampton Institute and started working as a full-time graphologist in 1990. And I have never looked back!

My work has been extremely varied and I have been lucky enough to be called upon to analyse the handwriting of politicians, celebrities, royalty and a whole host of famous and infamous characters, including one of the Great Train Robbers, as well as a famous newspaper magnate who was worried I would blackmail him with my insight into his personality (I resisted). I have also assisted with the recruitment and restructuring of companies, I have given relationship and career guidance to individuals, worked at corporate parties and events and helped solve problematic issues for security companies.

I love every minute of what I do. The only downside is that I receive precious few handwritten cards from friends, who are worried that I will be analysing them. Even the birthday cards they send me are typed!

So what is graphology?

When we put pen to paper, our personality is there in every stroke and mark we make. Whether we are the type to shout from the rooftops to make ourselves heard, or the sort to cower in the corner, whether we're an altruist or a bully, our character is displayed for the unpicking. Handwriting analysis – graphology – penetrates the disguise that we hide behind, revealing what makes us tick and, ultimately, what makes each one of us who we are.

There are a few things that we really can't tell from handwriting: whether we are left- or right-handed, what gender we are and, despite popular opinion, what age we really are (so it's safe to carry on lying!). But other than that, graphology illustrates how we interact with the world and the people around us, and also how we cope with stress and express emotions. It can help us make decisions about our future, showing us our inner desires and even what jobs and partners may suit us best. As you'll see as you keep reading, the devil is in the detail, whether it's in the width of a stroke or the curliness of a 'g', the spaces between the letters or the pressure of a pen.

There are also some golden rules about graphology that you really should abide by at all times. These are:

1.   Never diagnose a physical or psychological condition. Bear in mind that handwriting can change depending on someone's mood, energy level and health. Prescribed medication and recreational drugs as well as alcohol can cause rhythmic disturbance in a normally regular, controlled writer.

2.   Be sensitive to people's feelings when giving your analysis and emphasise the more positive traits – this book should in no way lead to divorce, murder or family strife! Always be tactful and kind and respect their privacy.

3.   When making a judgement about a person's character, you will find that some traits appear contradictory to others. This is normal as no one is black and white, straightforward or clear-cut. What you should be doing is looking for consistent traits that crop up several times in order to build up a true picture of the writer's personality. Try not to look at a word or a sentence in isolation.

So grab your pencil, pen or quill and let the fun begin . . .

Exercise 1: The Real You

Write a few sentences in the space provided below. It is always preferable to avoid copying something from a book as this will slow down your natural writing speed. Make sure you are writing on a flat surface and not while sitting as a passenger in a moving vehicle.

Sign your name under the text.

This will be the 'Real You' sample which you will refer back to throughout the book when I ask you to.

Chapter 1

THE BRAINY BIT

When I tell people what I do for a living, I occasionally come across someone who'll say something like: 'Graphology? It's just mumbo jumbo isn't it, like fortune-telling or palm-reading?'

Annoying though that sort of comment is for a graphologist or even someone with enough knowledge to look at handwriting in a different way – which is certainly going to be you by the end of this book – it's worth understanding how graphology actually works so as to give a convincing answer.

Handwriting, as with all fine motor coordination, is a physical process; the brain sends signals to the arm, the hand and the fingers to manipulate a writing tool (the pen or pencil you are holding). The brain is very much the main control room (perhaps it would be more accurate to call it brain-writing rather than handwriting!). Handwriting can be described as the X-ray of the mind. It is therefore not surprising that no two handwritings are the same and they are as unique as a fingerprint.

Your handwriting style is so much part of you that if you lost your ability to use your normal writing hand and were forced to write with the other hand, for example, then eventually over time your brain would adapt and produce writing very similar to the original. Even if you had to learn to write with your mouth or foot, your writing would eventually imitate your original writing style.

Try writing with the opposite hand that you are used to. What does it look like? If you compare it to your 'Real You' sample on p. 4, do you notice

any pointers in common that make it still look like your normal writing?

Keep practising and see what happens.

Now this may be a bit trickier, but have a go at writing with a pen or pencil in your mouth (please don't swallow it). The more agile amongst you can try using a foot. If you are right-handed, does it feel right to use your right foot? Most people are right-handed and right-footed (they lead with the right foot when they walk) or left-handed and left-footed, but not everyone. Therefore even though you are right-handed you may still find writing with the left foot preferable to the right.

Is your signature, the very essence of 'you', unrecognisable or, once again, can you find similarities with the one you did on p. 4?

As children, we learn everything for the first time by copying and following a set of rules imposed by adults. It is exactly the same with handwriting. To start off, children's handwriting is generally restricted to producing legible writing so that teachers can read it. We call that 'copybook' writing.

Over time, and certainly once out of the confines of the classroom, most children experiment and learn to develop their own style and will deviate from the copybook style that they were taught.

It is these deviations from the copybook that makes a person's handwriting and graphology so fascinating.

The brain and the mind are subject to both conscious and subconscious forces, and every individual is affected by whatever is part of their fixed or sometimes inherited traits, such as IQ, temperament, etc., but also by their more fluid traits such as attitudes, moods and physical health.

Can you think of a list of fixed traits in your personality that you think you possess and another list of more transient traits? As you go through the book you can see if these are evident in your writing.

Even though we change and are affected by those around us, events in our life or by the time of day, our main characteristics change far less during a lifetime. A signature is still required on legal documents, wills and so on and this is because it is a fairly reliable stamp of authenticity.

Signatures are fascinating. Do you remember as a child practising your signature? This is all part of the process of establishing an identity. You might have been influenced by the child sitting next to you in class, or a sibling or parent. But in time you will have found one that works for you and remains the same.

Try to imitate a friend or family member's signature.

If you find it hard, try turning it upside down and visualise it as a picture or pattern and see if that makes it easier. This will instinctively take you out of your natural tendency to use your own handwriting characteristics when you are confronted with an individual letter stroke.

We will be talking more about signatures later on in the book, to find out why they reveal a rather different part of your personality than what might emerge from the main text.

So, is graphology a science or an art?

This is an interesting question and not a particularly easy one to answer. I always think it is an 'inexact science' in the same way all forms of psychology are. True, it uses a systematised knowledge of a combination of known traits. For example, if we took a thousand people whose stubbornness was a dominant facet of their personality and looked at their writing, we would be able to see threads of similarity.

Over the years the founders of handwriting analysis have kept careful records of their findings, which are the basis of what we use today. Since we very first developed the ability to write, there have been academics and historians who have taken great pains to analyse what is hidden in our individual handwriting styles.

Julius Caesar's writing was analysed by Suetonius Tranquillus. The eleventh-century Chinese were studying the meaning behind handwriting, and in seventeenth-century Europe Camillo Baldi, an eminent doctor and historian, published *The Means of Knowing the Habits and Qualities of a*

Writer from His Letters.

Since then Gainsborough, Goethe, Jung and Einstein have all commented on the 'art' of handwriting analysis.

Having said that, an experienced graphologist will have perfected a way of 'seeing' that relies on a very intuitive understanding of the individual. We will be looking at this in more detail in the next chapter. By the end of this book you will have developed this skill yourself.

Try asking a range of friends and family with different professions what they think about handwriting analysis. Do you find that the sceptics tend to be more scientific or creative by nature?

Handwriting

Subconscious Traits

Fixed

IQ APTITUDES

LEFT- OR RIGHT-HANDED

SURVIVAL INSTINCTS

Fluid

PHYSICAL HEALTH

MENTAL HEALTH

SEXUALITY

APPETITES

MEMORY

Conscious Traits

Fixed

IDENTITY

Fluid

THOUGHTS

FEELINGS

BEHAVIOUR

DRINK

DRUGS

Chapter 2

LEARNING TO LOOK

When I started studying graphology, I soon realised that I had spent most of my life making judgements about character from handwritten letters and envelopes that I had received (in the case of the latter, some of these judgements, of course, could have been fantasy and influenced by whatever was in the envelope – the difference between pocket money from a generous aunt or my maths school report).

Often our instincts are spot on, but why should this be?

In the same way that humans are pre-programmed to understand a little about body language and attitude to determine whether someone is friend or foe, distressed or happy, open or secretive, we can often detect the same set of characteristics from handwriting.

There are certain universal signals that we give off whatever our culture or background. You could say that handwriting is body language on paper.

Exercise 2: Learning to Look

Who is the most outgoing?

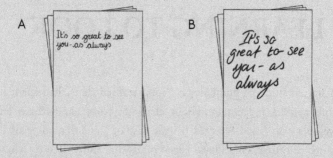

The answer is B. The writer has literally filled the page in an expansive way. The opposite is true of the timid, side-hugging A.

Who is the more aggressive?

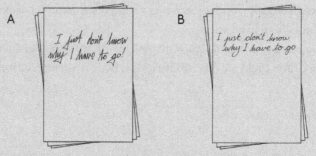

The answer is A. Look at the aggressive, angular strokes and the way that the writing looks determined, and even at times rather threatening.

Who is feeling more depressed?

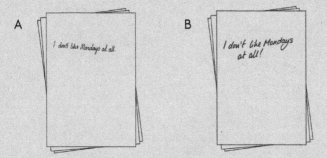

A   *I don't like Mondays at all.*

B   *I don't like Mondays at all!*

The answer is A. That drooping line just looks down and defeated as opposed to the upbeat, rising line of B.

Who hides their feelings more?

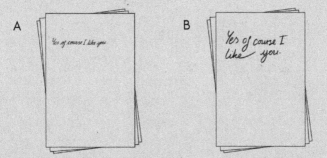

A   *Yes of course I like you*

B   *Yes of course I like you.*

The answer is A. The first thing that you notice is the smaller, more restrained, more cautious spacing and carefully made strokes of the letters.

Who is more tired?

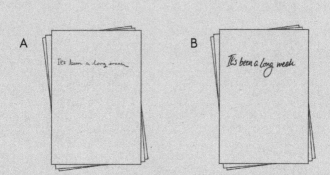

The answer is A. It looks like the writer barely has the energy to keep going across the page.

Which of these people do you think is more in love?

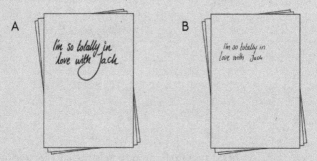

A again. The writing just looks more 'loved-up'. Jack seems to loom large in this person's life, and look at the telltale space before the name Jack in figure B. Is the writer pausing for thought?

Which of these newly marrieds is not altogether certain about their new family name?

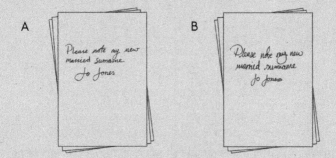

The answer is B. Look how Jo has used the last stroke of her new name to cross out 'Jones'. What do you think this may subconsciously mean?

Who isn't feeling well?

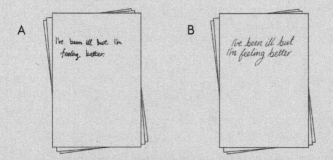

The answer is A. Look at the 'blotchy' and irregular script compared to the healthier example of B, which has more energy behind it.

Who is more likely to be telling the truth?

A

My name is Mary
and I'm   42 years
of age.

B

My name is Mary
and I'm 42 years
of age.

The answer is B. The first example shows Mary has left a very large space between 'I'm' and '42'. Why is she hesitating? Could it be that she's being creative with the truth?

Who is more difficult to get to know?

A

Hi let's move
a little closer.

B

Hi let's move a
little closer.

The answer is A. Those big spaces between the words look as though they spell distance, both physical and emotional!

The point of the exercises is to get you to use visual common sense and tap into your intuition when you first look at a sample of handwriting.

The things that leap out of the page at you are those traits that are definitely worth analysing further. What makes that first impression? What is out of kilter or what do you think the writer is trying to subconsciously emphasise or hide? Could a trait that is meant to catch your eye actually be a cover-up for something else? If we revert back to body language for a moment, would you always assume that someone with brightly coloured clothes is an extrovert or could they be trying to overcompensate for their lack of confidence?

As the Greek philosopher Plato said, 'Handwriting is the shackle of the mind'.

Certain aspects of graphology are based on logical psychological interpretations. As your knowledge increases, you will soon learn to see anything abnormal such as very large spaces in between the words in an otherwise tight handwriting or a particular word jumping off the baseline (see Chapter 4) as a clue that something is breaking the natural flow of the writer's thoughts.

Have a go at these and come to your own conclusions.

Dear Sir, I really want this job, not just because of the large Salary but because I just love the Banking world

I just wanted to let you know how happy I am now I have taken the job with Acme Security

yours sincerely

WHOSE LINE IS IT ANYWAY?

WHICH OF THESE INTERNATIONAL SUPERSTARS DO YOU THINK LOOKS THE MOST RELAXED?

Let's make it OURS

Beyoncé (signature)

the person
Leonardo DiCaprio (handwriting)

Beyoncé   Leonardo DiCaprio

ANSWER

Leonardo DiCaprio's handwriting and signature looks the more relaxed – look at the fluid slant and evenly spaced letters.

As your knowledge increases as you read this book, you will understand that he has written more speedily than Beyoncé, whose writing is more vertical with the use of slow and careful strokes.

In the following pages, we are going to go into depth and examine every facet of handwriting and each of the handwriting traits that makes up a unique individual.

Although we are going to examine each facet and trait at a time, please remember that we build up a picture of a personality by the slotting together of these elements. In other words, no one trait such as leftward slant or large size means much on its own. Everything is important but only when put together as a whole.

Chapter 3

THE ZONES

We all live in a three-dimensional world of height, width and depth. The way we write is a microcosm of how we relate to that world, with the upwards, downwards and sideways movement of our pen or pencil – the strokes – expressing something about our approach to life.

In handwriting, the letters of the alphabet span across three zones: the upper zone, the middle zone and the lower zone. Each zone has a different meaning and represents different psychological aspects of our personality. Whatever it is that you choose to write, be it a to-do list hurriedly pencilled on a scrap of paper or a graffiti that sweeps across a wall, the upper, middle and lower zones of your writing will always reveal something about you.

We can equate the three zones to the three sections of the human body: the head, the trunk and the legs. Interestingly, Sigmund Freud also divided the human psyche into three – the superego, the ego and the id. Both approaches roughly mirror the handwriting zone division below:

The upper zone – intellectual and spiritual matters.

The middle zone – relationships, emotions and day-to-day behaviour.

The lower zone – sexuality and materialistic concerns.

Look below to see which letters in the word 'flag' are present in which zone:

You will see that some small letters like 'a' and 'e' just stay in the middle zone, whereas the letter 't', for instance, travels across the upper and middle zone. Also, there is only one letter of the alphabet that normally spans all three zones and that is the letter 'f'.

UPPER-ZONE LETTERS

b d f h k l t

MIDDLE-ZONE LETTERS

a c e i m n o r s u v w x

LOWER-ZONE LETTERS

f g j p q y z

When you look at your own writing, it's likely that you will notice that your zones aren't even.

Which zone catches your eye? The upper, the middle or the lower one? Is there one that seems out of proportion or even missing altogether? If one zone is missing what do you think that might mean?

As with all things in life, a good healthy equilibrium is best, and so what most graphologists are looking for is a balance between the zones or anything that indicates the reverse of this.

Try writing out this sentence that includes all the letters of the alphabet: 'The quick brown fox jumps over the lazy dog'.

What do you deduce from what you have learned so far?

To go deeper, let's look at each zone in a little more detail.

The Upper Zone

The upper zone and the letters that stand tall, such as 'l' or 't', reflect our mental perceptions. They reveal how we think as opposed to how we act. All our intellectual and cultural aspirations are represented here.

This zone also points to our fantasy world, how we create illusions both for ourselves and other people. It denotes whether we have religious tendencies or strong spiritual or philosophical beliefs.

Emphasis on the upper zone can be a wonderful thing, but too much of it and people could see you as a flake, a dreamer or the ultimate trickster.

So how do we read and decode the characteristics of the upper zone?

Look back at your sentence. Examine how you formed the upper loops and strokes of the 'l's, 't's, 'f's, 'b's, 'h's, 'd's and 'k's.

In 'normal' upper zones, you should have well-proportioned loops and stems with reasonably placed 'i' dots and 't' crosses.

I was taught that 'perfect' handwriting consists of an upper and lower zone that are approximately twice the length of the middle zone. Copybook styles differ from country to country and certainly change from generation to generation.

I would love to speak to you about the books we spoke of

A healthy balance indicates mental capability, stability and an enquiring mind. If your writing looks anything like the sample above then you can breathe a sigh of relief, but don't panic if it doesn't. Most of us are not perfect (fortunately).

I dream about this every day and I just hate it.

An overly extended upper zone with long upward strokes that look out of place can denote someone who has reasonable intelligence and ambition but without the emotional maturity to bring their lofty ideas to fruition. This is the dreamer, the idealist.

If the upper-zone loops and strokes are so high that they begin to falter or distort, then this might be a warning sign of an extreme retreat into fantasy. This could be an individual disappointed by a life that never quite matches their expectations.

Of course there are some professions in which a dominant upper zone could be helpful, such as acting, writing, storytelling or indeed forgery.

Conversely, when the upper zone is short, this may indicate a writer who lacks creativity and imagination. Their interest is directed into the practical or physical areas of life, but they are also likely to be reliable and sociable.

Beware, though, of someone whose lower zone dominates their handwriting, as this is seen in graphology as a sign of greed – the writer may be dominated by their own need for physical satisfaction.

I'm happy not knowing what it is.

Now that we know what to look for in a dominant upper zone, there are some specific things to spot with upper-zone loops and strokes.

Sometimes upper-zone loops are overly inflated and look like balloons on a stick.

buy heaps of dollars

This kind of exaggeration is compensation for feelings of inferiority. The writer is constantly looking for reassurance and they may appear arrogant, boastful and even a little ridiculous. Their imagination and fantasy world may make them seem neurotic.

Some people have upper-zone formations that are completely free of embellishment. Such a person thrives on facts and concrete data. I doubt if they'd be one to indulge in small talk.

I like to say it how it is

If an upper-zone stroke has been subconsciously retraced to make the stroke look darker and firmer on the page then this is a sign of inhibition in the area of intellect, imagination and spirituality. Perhaps this writer's feelings and needs have been ridiculed in the past, making them feel insecure.

it was a shame not to be there

Upper-zone 'thrusting' is when the pen plunges dramatically from another zone of the handwriting into the upper zone. This is the sign of a keen mind, of someone who uses their creative and mental ability on a day-to-day basis.

However, moderation is key to all things successful and if there are too many thrusts, then this person may just be a little too eager to show their perceived intelligence. This, of course, makes for a successful showman or actor, but a potentially dull dinner guest.

Though I've been described as boring

When one line runs into another and tangling occurs, the messiness of the page may be reflecting confusion and clutter that exists in the writer's mind. There can be oodles of charm and charisma to this type of personality and they can be extremely creative, but they often need help in deciphering their thoughts.

I can't decide what to do at this time but it could work

Pointy tops to the upper-zone letters show an intelligent writer, but also someone who may perceive themselves as a little superior to others. This is certainly someone who finds it harder than most to take orders. It can be lonely at the top of a mountain . . .

I'm so glad to be top of the class

Some people form little circles as opposed to loops on their upper-zone letters. There is normally much originality and a good sense of humour in this kind of character.

I heard him laugh

If you see writing that has breaks in the upper-zone loops it could indicate that the writer feels they are literally falling apart and are feeling confused about life. That, or the ink was running out . . .

Incidentally, don't panic if you see this in your own or others' handwriting because this sort of trait can be very transitory, for instance when we are stressed out or under pressure.

help me please

Exercise 3: The Upper Zone

Which writer lives in a fantasy world?

A *fluffy*   B *fluffy*

Answer: A

Which writer will get straight to the point?

A *tell me about it*   B *Tell me about it*

Answer: B

Which writer is under stress?

A *I'm fine*   B *I'm fine*

Answer: B

Now have a look at your writing – what does the upper zone say about you?

What does your upper zone say about you?

Is your upper zone tall?

YES → THIS CAN BE A SIGN OF INTELLIGENCE

NO → THIS IS A SIGN OF A LACK OF CREATIVITY

Are your upper zones loopy?

YES → YOU MAY BE PRONE TO EXAGGERATION

NO → THIS SHOWS AN INDEPENDENT AND ENQUIRING MENTALITY

Do you have no upper zone?

YES → YOUR DAY-TO-DAY ACTIVITIES ARE OFTEN MORE IMPORTANT TO YOU THAN INTELLECTUAL MATTERS.

Does your upper zone tangle with the middle zone?

YES → YOU MAY BE EASILY DISTRACTED AND OVERLY SENSITIVE

NO → THIS IS A SIGN OF A STRONG IMAGINATION

The Middle Zone

The central section of your handwriting delves into the sphere of the here and now. People who have dominant middle zones are rooted in the present and are concerned with practical and everyday concerns.

The strokes and shapes formed in the middle zone represent emotional expression, be it self-contained and cool, or a bubbling cauldron of angst. On top of this, it also reflects our work and practical activity.

Because this zone is about day-to-day issues, it is one that is likely to fluctuate – sometimes even on an hourly basis, which of course makes for fascinating analysis. Try writing a sentence in the morning, for example, and see if it's any different if you write that same sentence in the evening.

A medium-height middle zone that neither dominates nor is swamped entirely by the upper and lower zones indicates a healthy level of self-confidence (turn to my comment on p. 19 about the 'perfect' ratio).

Someone with a balanced middle zone is probably someone with a sensible attitude to life in general.

I am very normal indeed

A very large middle zone that appears dominant over the upper and lower zones indicates someone who tends towards self-interest. Other factors in the handwriting will determine someone's sensitivity, but if there is a very large middle zone then it's quite likely that they're the sort of person who is impulsive and who simply cannot wait when they want something.

tending to have my own way

Often this person might come across as immature and selfish. Young people and children naturally tend to have large middle zones.

A middle zone can also be very small indeed, to the extent that it seems dwarfed by the other two zones.

my personality is not equal to yours

Despite the outwardly confident appearance of this writer (look at that upper zone), the reality is that this person really feels inferior and underrates their own abilities.

If a small middle zone is in proportion to a small upper and lower zone and the letters look legible and well formed, then this may be an independent spirit who's in possession of excellent powers of concentration. Not a bad way to be.

One way of determining how moody or temperamental a person may be is by looking at the regularity of the size of the middle zone.

A fluctuating middle-zone size indicates a more tricky personality that is quick to become emotionally attached. People may find this individual exhausting and difficult to fathom. However, he or she may also be a very versatile individual and unlikely to be boring!

independent of spirit and happy with my own company.

A jerky middle zone, sometimes with the odd break in the stroke, can be a danger sign (we will be covering danger signs in detail in another chapter). This jerkiness could just be passing tension or stress, but regular snags in the writing can indicate a chronic physical condition or psychological problem. Of course, age should be taken into account: a tremulous hand is quite normal in an octogenarian but not so normal for someone in their twenties or thirties.

However, do remember – never diagnose a physical or psychological condition – you are not qualified to do so . . .

he wanted my help but not really

We have talked about tangles in the upper zone, but tangling in the middle zone can also occur and betray the fact that this person tends to take on more than they can handle, and that their everyday life is chaotic and undisciplined.

now is not the time

I'm sure you have spotted writers who have very tightly closed or even looped middle-zone letters, as in the examples below. This indicates someone who is good at keeping secrets but may be quite difficult to get to know as they are extremely private.

always secretive

Sometimes people even double loop their middle-zone ovals – look at the 'o's and the 'a's here. Good luck with getting information out of these people . . .

don't ask me about how

You'll have worked out that an oval that is completely open denotes a chatterbox. Best not tell these people your darkest secrets! This lot can't resist passing on news and information.

I love to communicate!

Exercise 4: The Middle Zone

Which writer is the more childlike?

A *I love playing*   B I Love playing

Answer: B

Which of these is the more moody writer?

A *yes and no*   B *yes and no*

Answer: A

And back to the sentence you wrote at the beginning of this chapter: how does your middle zone compare to the upper and lower zone? Are you mainly driven by your ego or are your thoughts on a higher level?

Have a good look and now see how difficult it is to change the size of your middle zone. How does it make you feel when you force yourself to change?

What does your middle zone say about you?

Is your middle zone large?

YES

THIS CAN BE
A SIGN OF A
LARGE EGO.

*Is it in proportion
with upper and lower zone?*

YES

YOU HAVE GREAT
POWERS OF
CONCENTRATION

NO

YOU MAY BORE
OTHERS WITH YOUR
SELF-INTEREST!

NO

THIS CAN BE A SIGN
OF GOOD CONCENTRATION

*Are your ovals
tightly closed?*

YES

YOU ARE SECRETIVE
AND DISCRETE

NO

Are they open?

YES

YOU FIND IT HARD
TO KEEP A SECRET

NO

ARE YOU AN
ACCOUNTANT?

The Lower Zone

This is where it gets interesting. If I'm giving a talk or presentation this is invariably the area of the handwriting which creates the most interest and often forces my talk to overrun. Why? Because the lower zone relates to our unconscious and instinctual urges; our downward strokes and movements under the baseline indicate our material needs and wants. They show us how important we think money and all that it can buy is.

Governed by sensual perception, the lower zone also covers our basic human drives, which include sex and materialism.

As the lower zone is all about the unconscious drives that make us human, it covers a lot of things that most people want to keep private. But it's not easy to keep a secret from a graphologist . . .

A normal well-balanced lower zone tends to be slightly longer than the upper zone, with perhaps a little more room for variety of form. All in all, it should look in keeping with the rest of the writing and not be overly embellished.

looking forward to seeing you.

If the lower-zone loops and strokes seem to dominate the whole writing and your eyes are drawn to . . . well . . . down below, then the writer may find it difficult to control their physical impulses.

I love swinging parties

If the lower zone is so exaggerated that it becomes entangled with the other lines of the handwriting, then this may indicate a writer who is a little too confused to get much fun out of their physical life.

I enjoy being around lots of people so that I got

When the lower zones are rather stunted the physical part of life is rarely of much importance to the writer.

If the lower-zone figures are short and stick-like this can point to a practical thinker who doesn't allow themselves to get caught up in unconscious desires.

I'm happy to be very determined and organised

This sort of control can make someone very precise indeed. Too blunt and this could indicate more of a cruel mind.

If the lower-zone loops are retraced, this can be a sign of repression in the realm of relationships. It can be difficult to get close to this person on any level.

I keep myself to myself

Some writers make long stick-like figures with their lower-zone letters. The additional length shows a restless character who can be defensive. They like to draw a wall around themselves to avoid any danger of being hurt. They are very aware of their instinctual drives but fear losing themselves in the process.

I need to forget you quickly

Triangular shapes in the lower zone are quite cumbersome and slow to form but that doesn't seem to stop some people making them. Here we may be looking at someone who is happy to be judgmental about other people's private lives while guarding their own like the crown jewels.

I don't get drunk easily like you.

Most of us, in fact, have a combination of the lower-zone characteristics listed above, but occasionally flip-flopping between a wide variety of lower-zone forms can hint at an unsettled sexual focus, perhaps even an insatiable appetite . . .

Please buy out my interest as I'm very busy just about every day

Careful now . . .

Exercise 5: The Lower Zone

Is this writer more interested in Rory, Sally or Milly?

I like Rory Sally and Milly

Answer: Sally

Which writer has the stronger instinctual drive?

A *I'm working for money*

B *I'm working) for money)*

Answer: B but . . .

Do you think that Sample B is the writer with the stronger instincts or could the exaggeration point to compensation for something that is lacking?

As you go through the book, you will learn to spot telltale compensatory signs.

What does your lower zone say about you?

Does your Lower zone dominate your writing?

YES → YOU MAY POSSESS A STRONG PHYSICAL DRIVE

NO → YOU ARE THE PRACTICAL AND RELIABLE SORT

YES branch:

Is your lower zone loopy?

YES → YOU COULD BE A LITTLE GREEDY

NO → YOU CAN BE SENSITIVE TO OTHERS BUT FEAR LOSING YOURSELF TO YOUR OWN NEEDS

Does your Lower zone tangle with the Middle zone?

YES → YOUR OWN NEEDS AND DESIRES INTERFERE WITH DAILY LIFE

NO → YOU HAVE A STRONG PHYSICAL AND SEXUAL SIDE BUT A HEALTHY REGARD FOR OTHERS

Is your writing pressure overly strong and heavy?

THIS MAY BE A DANGER SIGN FOR AGGRESSION

NO branch:

Is your Lower zone very short?

YES → A SIGN OF LOW PHYSICAL DRIVE

NO → YOU'RE WELL BALANCED

Zonal Balance

This does not refer to a new form of extreme yoga, but shows us how all of the characteristics of our zones interact with one another to reflect a personality.

Zonal balance highlights how we handle our thoughts and feelings, our expressions and ultimately our goals and desires.

Do we have inner equilibrium or does our ego squash otherwise intelligent decision-making?

DOMINANT UPPER ZONE

I make things up

DOMINANT MIDDLE ZONE

big egos rock

DOMINANT LOWER ZONE

I'm very physical

It's not surprising that a healthy balance between all three zones is the ideal. Overemphasis in any one zone invariably points to the fact that it is at the expense of one or more areas of your life.

Look at the writing in your sentence and see what you can deduce from the three different zones of your handwriting. Write the same sentence again and see if your writing has changed.

If it has, do you think it is because you are just in a different frame of mind, or are you much more self-conscious about achieving a zonal balance?

WHOSE LINE IS IT ANYWAY?

What can you detect so far about these well-known people's personalities from what you have learned in this chapter?

Victoria Beckham

Donald Trump

William Shakespeare

Marie Curie

Jackie Kennedy

Here are my thoughts. Have a read and see whether my analyses match yours.

Victoria Beckham

This celebrity and fashion designer shows a tall upper zone as well as strokes in the middle zone that plunge right down into the lower-zone section. The middle zone itself stays steady and small.

Victoria has a healthy sense of pride in her accomplishments and is creative in her ideas. She can be a little stubborn, but her ego is healthy without being dominating and she has a well-balanced view of life.

Donald Trump

The President of the USA has a strong middle zone which appears to be the dominant zone. Both the upper and lower zones are shorter and largely unembellished.

Donald Trump has a strong ego, and everyday concerns including his presidential role are likely to take precedence over his intellectual and physical life, which are both undertaken with control.

What do you think the extreme vertical slant of his handwriting may mean? It almost looks as though he has used a ruler to keep his letters very rigid and straight?

Do you think this means that he is likely to be influenced by others' opinions or does he rely on his own instincts?

(I think the latter, don't you?)

William Shakespeare

Shakespeare is a world-renowned playwright but what does his handwriting tell us?

It is dominated by a very strong lower zone which at times tangles up with the writing, which makes it look rather a mess.

If you look carefully you will also see that there appears to be quite a wide variety of loops and lower-zone formations.

Mr Shakespeare had a more than healthy physical drive and a very restless and febrile personality. He was still able to produce a prodigious number of influential plays and poems that are recognised as such even hundreds of years after his life.

Marie Curie

This famous physicist and chemist possessed a healthy balance between all three zones, but if you look carefully you will see that there is evidence of some retracing in the lower zone.

She has a good balance between the down-to-earth reality of science and a strong imagination, which would have helped her to realise her ground-breaking discoveries.

The retraced lower zone indicates that Marie may have found personal relationships more difficult to maintain.

Jackie Kennedy

This former presidential First Lady and international fashion icon has a dominant upper zone which appears to loom high above the other two zones.

Jackie shows enormous pride as well as a religious devotion in life. She is emotional but also vulnerable, as her sense of dignity and pride attempts to balance out her feelings of insecurity, betrayed in her undersized middle zone. She was able to tolerate the constraints of life in the White House thanks to her fertile imagination.

As we know from the many interviews she gave, she certainly exuded charm and charisma and could hold her own in any intellectual arena.

Chapter 4

THE BASELINE

The baseline is the imaginary line that we write on when we use a blank piece of paper.

When children first learn to write, it is difficult for them to keep to a straight line so they learn on lined paper. Adults tend not to use lined paper, and you can tell a lot about a writer's moods and attitudes from the imaginary baseline that they have constructed for themselves.

Try writing a few lines of handwriting on a blank piece of paper. Now draw a line under the middle-zone letters and look to see how straight or wavy your baseline looks. Is it rigid, gently undulating or is it all over the place?

In Western writing we can imagine the piece of paper to be a road that is travelled on from left to right, with the left representing the past and the right representing the future. The route that we take to move across the paper is an indication of our subconscious journey and, in particular, what controls and disciplines we use or don't use to achieve our goals.

When you are asking someone to give you a sample of their handwriting, always ask them to write on unlined paper. You do not want a sample from someone who feels hemmed in – they should be free to create their own 'picture'. What do you think it means if someone actually chooses to write on lined paper? Do you know someone like that?

In body language, it is a universal given that 'up' is better than 'down' and that someone who walks around with drooped shoulders is likely to be more depressed than the upright, head-up-straight walker. We use words such as 'feeling down', 'chin up!' and even 'on the straight and narrow'.

The same can be said for handwriting, especially in terms of baseline, as you will find out below. Just be aware that if the paper isn't straight to begin with, then you may get a false upward or downward slope.

Normal Straight Line

I am dependable and mostly composed so that I know what

This person is stable and controlled. Unless other factors in the handwriting say otherwise, then a normal but not overly rigid baseline is a sign of dependability and a person who is likely to allow their head to rule their heart.

Overly Rigid Baseline

I never deviate and I stay in control all of the time

Some people write as though they have used an imaginary ruler. This implies they have enormous control over their pen (and therefore, one would deduce, of their environment).

This could be a bit of a warning sign that you have come across a control freak, needing rigid order and structure. This trait can also be an indication that the writer in fact feels out of control and compensates by exerting some kind of influence over less important aspects of their life.

It takes a lot of hard work to write like this – a slow and arduous process. Later in the book we will discuss speed of writing, but rest assured that there is a lack of spontaneity here that should ring alarm bells (more about this in Chapter 17, 'Danger Signs').

Ascending Baseline

I just know today is going to be great

An ascending baseline will have every word rising like a hill to the other side of the page. As we have seen at the beginning of this chapter, it is nearly always a positive sign and means that the writer is feeling optimistic, happy with life and generally upbeat.

Of course, these feelings can change like the wind, but if the writer has an upward slant as a regular theme to their writing then you can be assured that they are rarely discouraged, have tenacity of purpose and are great at working as part of a team.

However, as with all things, nothing should be too extreme and so, if the writing is severely sloping up, then they may just be a little too upbeat when realism is called for!

Descending Baseline

It's been quite difficult recently to stay afloat and I've been concerned.

The droopy or descending baseline immediately looks unhappy and downcast.

No prizes for guessing that the writer is not feeling great about themselves; perhaps life has taken a downward turn or they just aren't feeling well.

It may be a one-off, but if this is a regular feature it may mean that the writer looks on the negative side of life and may be caught up in their own gloom.

Flexible Baseline

I'm feeling pretty excited about things because it's a busy time

Most of us exhibit a flexible baseline from time to time, especially when we are writing fast. This means that we are open to the ideas of others and at the time of writing feel excitable and energetic. It might be that our mood is a little unstable. Either way we are open and receptive to all that is going on around us.

Extremely Erratic Baseline

I can't make up my mind as I need to know where I stand

This is more unusual but nevertheless points to a writer who is extremely emotional, feels confused and lacks the necessary willpower and strength to make good decisions.

Again, remember that this could be a very transitory trait. Also, one too many glasses of wine or tiredness can also result in erratic baselines, so don't be too quick to judge yourself or others!

False Ascending Baselines

I can't wait to see you in the morning because I haven't seen you

Be on the lookout for baselines that start on an upward swing and then level out. The writer starts communicating with optimism but is unable to maintain it – I think we all know people like this.

The Falling-off-at-the–End Baseline

I'm hoping I can make it but it's been a long week and I know that

This is similar to the above, except that the writer starts with a fairly level baseline, then each line droops sometimes quite strongly at the end of each line.

The writer could just be tired and finding it difficult to keep going, but on the other hand it could be indicative of poor planning. If they can't judge the end of the paper then they are unlikely to have good planning ability for other aspects of their life.

Very occasionally this trait seen regularly could point to a more chronically unhappy writer.

The Convex Baseline

I would like to come out to play and see you sometime

This may look like an extreme version of what we've just looked at, but if the lines on the page look like a downturned mouth then the writer feels that life can be disappointing and may have a tendency to give up on ideas, projects or even people too easily. Can you see anything else in the writing that may indicate this?

The Concave Baseline

I sometimes lose the plot but then I think, 'come on – you can do it!'

The reverse of the convex points to a writer whose initial enthusiasm can wane, but then they have the ability to pick themselves up and carry on with gusto. Perhaps more of the long-distance runner than the sprinter, this is certainly someone who has the ability to work hard and reach their targets in life.

Ascending Baseline Steps

I'm sure things will be great because I will win

Sometimes you see this pattern in just the odd line, or occasionally a writer will create a whole letter in this way.

The individual words look as though they are tiles on a roof and have an upward slant. He or she is aware that they need to keep a check on their excitement or enthusiasm, and they are trying hard to control their emotions.

Descending Steps Baseline

I hope that it will work
but its hard to be optimistic

This has the same 'tiling' effect, but now the tiles or words are descending. The writer is fighting a negative attitude and, depending on the subject matter or whatever is on their mind, they may not be feeling optimistic.

Specific-Word(s)-Rise Baseline

I like them both:
Harry has his good
points but John

This can be fun: look at the actual word that is higher than the others. There will be a reason behind why that object, thought, action or person is uppermost in the writer's mind. John is clearly a popular fellow in this writer's mind . . .

Specific-Word(s)-Fall Baseline

I had a great time
last night.

A mirror-image to the specific-word-rise baseline, this is easy to spot and interpret. The writer appears to have a negative feeling about the word. What is the word and why would this be? Possibly because they are fooling themselves, but – as you are finding out – it's much harder to fool a graphologist!

Exercise 6: Baselines

Who is feeling more optimistic?

A   *Have a great day*   B   *Have a great day.*

Answer: A

Who is moodier?

A   *Please can you let me know when you are*   B   *Please can you let me know when you are.*

Answer: B

Who is looking forward to the party?

A   *I can't wait to see you at the party*   B   *I can't wait to see you at the party*

Answer: A

What is on this person's mind?

*I would like my handwriting analysed
All aspects of career, love, money*

Answer: Love

Now go back to your 'Real You' sample and assess how you think your baseline looks and what it says about you when you wrote it. Can you compare it to something you wrote in the past? Is there a difference and, if so, why would this be?

Try writing out the same sentence at different times of the day and see if the baseline remains the same.

Now find letters that have been written to you and work out how the writer was really feeling when he or she wrote them.

I have had letters from friends and acquaintances that I consider to be happy upbeat people, only to observe that they are hiding anxiety at that particular period in their lives, and it shows up in their baselines.

Just for fun, try writing a line or two with a ruled line rigidly marking the baseline. How does this make you feel, and do you like the look of the end result? If you do then it may point to a love of order and control you didn't know you had.

What does your _baseline_ say about you?

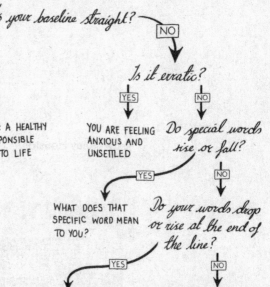

Is your baseline straight?

YES →

Is it rigid?

YES → YOU MAY BE A CONTROL FREAK

NO → YOU HAVE A HEALTHY AND RESPONSIBLE OUTLOOK TO LIFE

NO →

Is it erratic?

YES → YOU ARE FEELING ANXIOUS AND UNSETTLED

NO → **Do special words rise or fall?**

YES → WHAT DOES THAT SPECIFIC WORD MEAN TO YOU?

NO → **Do your words drop or rise at the end of the line?**

YES → YOUR ENTHUSIASM OR CURRENT MOOD MAY NOT BE SUSTAINABLE

NO → YOU HAVE A HEALTHY AND FLEXIBLE ATTITUDE TO LIFE WITHOUT BEING RIGID

WHOSE LINE IS IT ANYWAY?

Here are three variations of baseline from three very different well-known figures. What conclusions can you draw about their personalities based on their baselines?

Whitney Houston

Queen Elizabeth I

Michael Jackson

Whitney Houston

Whitney Houston has written and signed with a very upward rising slant. The handwriting is also extravagant and large and she has even 'finale'd with a smiley face!

Whitney was feeling upbeat, enthusiastic and optimistic when she wrote this one.

Queen Elizabeth I

Notwithstanding that this is of course an archaic way of writing, complete with curlicues and written with a quill, you will see that the baseline is straight in the extreme and this person has taken great care to write slowly and with precision.

Queen Elizabeth I was not known for her extreme flexibility on certain matters and she will have become accustomed to a life of discipline, order and formal dignity that would have called upon superhuman levels of control and loyalty to tradition. I think all those traits are evident here!

Michael Jackson

By comparison, the singer Michael Jackson has written with baselines that appear to swoop downwards and with downward tiling. Michael was clearly not feeling too good about himself when he wrote this and it was difficult for him to maintain a positive outlook.

Chapter 5

SLANT

One of the questions that I am repeatedly asked when people learn that I am a graphologist is 'Isn't a left slant really bad?' or even 'Does a left slant mean that you're dishonest/bad/mad?'

The fact is that in the Western world we are taught to write from left to right, and a moderate right slant means that for 90 per cent of us we are less likely to smear the page with ink.

For the other 10 per cent or thereabouts that are left-handed, unless they hold their pen with their hand curled round, then they are at risk of getting inky, smudgy hands.

Nevertheless both right- and left-handed writers can have a left slant, which would certainly be going against the 'norm' by copybook standards, or at least would indicate a subconscious decision to go against how they were taught.

Does this mean they are antisocial, intrinsically different or just oddballs? Well, it certainly doesn't mean they are by default mad, bad or untrustworthy.

The slant of the handwriting, whether forward, backward or rigidly vertical, is an indication of how we express our emotions to others and the outside world. In short, it can reveal how sociable or unsociable we appear to be.

Slant is interesting for a graphologist because it is the graphological movement that is most prone to change with stress, mood or life experience.

Over the years, as our confidence or ability to bounce back from adversity increases, slant can change to reflect this.

When I was studying I learned to measure slant with a special instrument to gauge the exact degree of incline, but you can make some great observations just by using the naked eye.

The Vertical Slant

I tend not to panic because
I keep my head

If you see a piece of handwriting without a left or right slant, but more of a vertical one, this is an indication of someone who uses diplomacy and reason over emotion to get through life. Definitely a 'head over heart' kind of person.

They are the ones to rely on in a crisis and often make excellent leaders, able to keep calm when others lose their heads. There is an inner strength to them which may not make them the life and soul of the party, but they'll know the quickest, panic-free route out when the party venue catches fire.

Overly Rigid Slant

Totally in control

Have you ever seen a sample of writing that looks as though someone has used a ruler to draw the downstrokes? It's so rigid that its very presence on the page makes you sit up and pay attention.

I'm not saying they have control issues and are likely to live their life in an extremely disciplined manner (actually, yes I am).

It takes immense effort to keep to such a rigid stroke.

Normal Right Slant

I'm a good mixer and love to see my friends

It feels altogether more comfortable to write with a slight right slant, which gives a visual feeling of forward movement without excessive haste or wobble.

Logical but emotional, this writer can show both compassion and empathy without dissolving into tears at the drop of a hat.

Very Inclined Right Slant

I was so upset when she didn't get back to me.

These people wear their heart on their sleeve. Affectionate and extremely sensitive, they may burst into tears or hysterical laughter at the slightest thing. Walking on eggshells springs to mind.

If the slant is so inclined that it is almost horizontal then think 'volcano' – passionate, jealous and perhaps even prone to emotional fantasy. Crikey!

Reclined Slant

I can take it or leave
It really.

Always note that it often feels more natural for a left-handed person to write with a slight left slant (to avoid the smudge factor) which is why I will always ask if someone is right- or left-handed before analysing. Sometimes it's not possible to know and if this is the case do use caution when judging a slight left slant.

Left-handers aside, the fact of the matter is that most of us feel more comfortable with a right slant, so what does it mean if we choose to be different?

The left slant can mean a repression of feeling while the writer attempts to figure out which bit of their personality they feel most comfortable sharing with the rest of the world. Interestingly, it's not uncommon for teenagers to have a left slant before settling into a different slant when they are older.

Often, a left-leaning handwriting points to someone resisting change, progress or authority. In other words, these writers see themselves as something of a maverick.

Very Reclined Slant

I keep thinking about
yesterday.

A very reclined slant can look rather unnatural and tends to belong to a person who is more self-orientated and lives more in the past. Occasionally you will come across a slant that is so laid back it has almost fallen flat on its back. This can indicate extreme self-interest. It can also point to deception: be on your guard.

Have a look at writing samples that describe past events and you may find that the writer leans a little more to the left than he or she normally would.

Unstable Slant

Sometimes I think one thing and sometimes another

Handwriting slant can vary to a lesser or greater degree even within the same piece of writing, but if you're someone with a highly changeable slant, this can point to moodiness and emotional unreliability. I think I'll leave it there!

Specific Slant Peccadilloes

Sometimes you will see a change in slant which highlights an individual word or line. As we have seen with anomalies in the section about zonal balance, have a look to see what it is the writer is getting fired up about:

you are great in bed

or concerned about:

I was unhappy to see you looking sad.

Exercise 7: Slant

Try writing something that you really don't believe. Do you hate tomatoes? If so, write down that they are your favourite food. See if your slant is the same as in your 'Real You' sample.

Polygraph tests may reveal the anxiety in our physical bodies when we tell a lie, but handwriting can reveal the same from deep within our subconscious.

Who do you think you would feel more comfortable being friends with?

I'd really like us to be friends

I'd really like us to be friends

I'd really like us to be friends

Now compare the writing to your own. Can you see why one or even two of these might put you off being friends with this writer – and might even make you feel unnerved? Not everyone will feel the same, but you are well on the way to seeing how the psychological aspects of graphology can help with compatibility, which we will explore in depth in Chapter 19.

Do you think these two people would get on?

A   *I really hope they like me*

B   I'm totally cool with it

The answer is almost certainly a no!

Writer A is very emotional, wears their heart on their sleeve and is even a little needy, requiring reassurance and compliments. Writer B, on the other hand, is much more self-contained and private.

A would find B a cold fish and B would be scared off by A's emotional fragility.

C   I'm here if you need me

The person who is likely to get on with both A and B is C.

Neither a hothead nor an ice maiden, this writer keeps their head and can show strong diplomatic tendencies. A job in the diplomatic service beckons, I feel.

To assess your own slant, write out the following sentence:

Pack my box with six dozen liquor jugs.

Now take a pencil and a ruler and extend your upper-zone letters. This should give you a clearer idea of what sort of slant you have.

Now do the same with the letters with the lower-zone strokes – the 'y', the 'q', the 'j' and the 'g'.

Is there a marked difference in the slant of the different zones? What do you think that might say about you?

Try writing out the same sentence with the hand you don't normally use. Does your slant change and do you think that over time it would revert to looking like your normal handwriting ?

I love people so much

keeping things straight

happy alone keeping my distance

Find a lengthy example of your writing – a letter or perhaps an essay. Look closely. Can you spot any words or letters that stand out because they have a different slant from the rest of the writing? Why would that be?

As in the middle zone exercise on p. 29, write a sentence in the morning when you first wake up and then write the very same sentence just before you go to bed. Has there been a change in slant, and in what direction?

What does your <u>slant</u> say about you?

Is your slant vertical?

YES

YOU ARE A PERSON IN
CONTROL OF YOUR EMOTIONS

NO

Does it slant to the right?

YES

NO

Does it have a <u>very</u> inclined slant?

Is it slightly reclined?

YES

YOU FIND IT HARD TO
HIDE YOUR EMOTIONS AND
CAN BE A LITTLE NEEDY...

NO

YOU HAVE A HEALTHY
EMOTIONAL OUTLOOK
ON LIFE

YES

YOU KEEP YOUR
COOL UNDER
PRESSURE BUT
CAN GET STUCK
IN THE PAST

NO

IF YOUR SLANT
IS <u>VERY</u> RECLINED
IT CAN INDICATE
DIFFICULTY IN
RELATING TO
OTHERS

WHOSE LINE IS IT ANYWAY?

Take a look at these two famous twentieth-century artists. Judging by the slant of their handwritings, do you think they would get on if they had met?

Andy Warhol

Salvador Dalí

Andy Warhol

The artist Andy Warhol shows a gentle right slant to the writing which shows he has a healthy need to communicate, even though other factors in this sample indicate that he is highly intuitive and sensitive.

Salvador Dalí

The more flamboyant Dalí shows a mixed slant to his writing, demonstrating his unpredictable emotions and febrile mind, as well as his highly unusual creativity.

In fact the two did meet in a hotel in the summer of 1965. History records that Warhol was caught off guard by the theatrical encounter with the painter, and his photographer described it as five 'uncomfortable minutes'.

However, Andy Warhol was still mesmerised enough by the man to return several times to seek out his company even though their styles of both art and communication were clearly very different.

Chapter 6

PRESSURE AND BREADTH

As a graphologist I am not always able to choose the nature of the handwriting sample that I analyse. However, if I do have a choice I prefer an original sample, not a photocopy or scan.

The reason for this is that the pressure we exert on the paper can be very revealing about our mental energy, our appetites and desires, as well as our physical drive and health.

The best way of judging pressure is to turn the paper over and feel with your finger the indentation, if any, that the writer has created with his or her pen.

Is the paper quite smooth? Has the pen pressure left ridges that you can feel or is the pressure so extreme that it has even ripped the paper (a rare occurrence, but I've seen it!)? Some writing instruments are better at showing pressure than others. The good old pencil and the biro are better than a roller ball. When it isn't possible to look at the original sample, the darkness of a stroke can give some indication of pressure, and, by extension, of what we're all about.

Do bear in mind that pressure can change frequently depending on state of mind and health and even how much we have had to drink. An experienced graphologist will refrain from judging someone's character by their pen pressure unless it appears to be a consistent feature and samples written over a period of time can be compared.

'Normal' Pressure

As you become familiar with looking at your own and others' handwriting you will learn to look at the 'breadth' of the handwriting as well as the depth, i.e. pressure.

'Normal' – not really a word that I like to use very often – means that the strokes do not catch the eye, they are neither strong and visually dark, nor are they particularly light. Incidentally, it is 'normal' to have slightly heavier pressure exerted on the downstrokes, i.e. when your pen is moving away from the top of the page as opposed to bringing your pen in an upward movement or when making a horizontal stroke such as a 't' bar, so don't focus too much on that.

feeling just fine

This person shows both mental and physical health.

Heavy Pressure

I just wont put up with it!

Heavier pressure looks, feels and in fact is, more intense. The writer may be feeling determined to get their point across and even a little angry. If heavy pressure seems to be a permanent feature of someone's handwriting then this would certainly indicate someone who would use all their energy to get what they want.

Depending on other aspects of the handwriting, he or she may be dynamic and vital or just plain aggressive.

Very Heavy Pressure

Get out of my way!

When very heavy pressure is applied, the underside of the paper should feel extremely textural. Look out for rips!

This individual could be overly ambitious in all or part of his or her life, opinionated and sometimes quite brutal. Look to see if there is any one zone in which the pressure is particularly heavy. Is there an area of life where the aggression is more dominant? Intellectual (upper), domestic (middle) or sexual (lower)? We will be covering the negative side of very heavy pressure in more detail in Chapter 17.

It is worth noting that some medications and certain health issues can result in a heavier than normal pressure, so don't be too quick to judge.

Light Pressure

I had a great massage.

If the handwriting seems quite light in colour and there has been little or no mark on the reverse of the paper, then we can say that the writer has light pressure.

This writer is likely to be sensitive and impressionable, and easy to get on with – a follower rather than a leader. They may have quite a creative or spiritual nature, but do they have the tenacity to follow through with their dreams? That might be a relevant question.

Very Light Pressure

I'm a little frightened

If the pressure is so light that it is hard to read and looks as though it is literally 'fading' as you look at it, this reveals a character full of self-doubt, lacking in willpower and possibly physical vitality.

Uneven Pressure

I'm worried

Uneven pressure is the sign of a worrier, someone who churns events over in their mind. As with all indications of handwriting that isn't regular or smooth, the uneven pressure shows a certain nervousness to the personality. Imagine someone pacing a room, stopping, pausing, then pacing speedily forward again . . .

Pasty Writing

Some handwritings look 'pasty' because the stroke is rather thick and each movement has produced a lot of ink. Of course, various writing instruments make pasty writing almost inevitable, for instance when using a felt-tip pen. However, if the writing is consistently 'pasty' or consistently rather 'thin' and sparse-looking, then this too has a meaning. Remember, in graphology *nothing* is wasted!

I want you now!

The writing above looks blobby and each stroke is broad. Some of the ovals have even been filled with ink.

Certainly this writer is sensually driven. Of course, this quality can produce great artists and musicians but it can also produce individuals that are driven by their physical needs. I think we all know what I'm hinting at . . .

Too pasty and exploding with ink is a danger sign – too much passion can also equate to too much anger and too many explosions of temper.

Sharp Writing

I can't I'm too scared

If you come across a writing that looks 'sharp' and narrow and rather 'clean'-lined it can indicate a very reserved and cautious individual.

The intellect can be sharp too if there are other indications (remember that upper zone?) but it can also suggest someone rather aloof and precious.

A Word on Pen Choice

I have already mentioned that the felt-tip pen causes a broader stroke than the biro by default, but what does it mean when someone actually chooses a particular type of writing instrument?

The Felt Tip

The felt tip is a terrible writing instrument to use if you are having your character analysed because there is no way to see pressure, shading or any individual minutiae of strokes.

So why would you choose to write with one? Maybe because you just love its big brash strokes, which you can make with minimal effort. I'm not saying you are narcissistic and lazy, but well . . . What do you think?

The Ballpoint Pen

The ballpoint user likes to leave a clear, clean, no-nonsense mark on the paper. These qualities are likely to be reflected in the personality too, but conversely it is often the nearest thing to hand when we want to write a shopping list or even write a letter.

The Fountain Pen

How I love my fountain pen! Sadly fewer people seem to use them these days and those that do tend to care very much about the way their letter looks. Because the fountain pen takes a little more effort to maintain, these people are likely to be fastidious and just a little bit old-fashioned.

The Pencil

The humble pencil is actually a great instrument for a graphologist because its stroke can really show up pressure and shading. Pencils are often used by people who want to correct their work without crossing out (yes, erasers still exist). Or maybe they are also people who fear commitment!

A pencil is cheap and handy to chew on. Analyse that as you will.

The Quill

Forget it . . .

Exercise 8 : Pressure

Who is the more anxious of these two?

A   It will be fine

B   It will be fine

It's A – look at that uneven pressure.

Who out of these two partygoers is likely to be the life and soul?

A   Loving the party

B   loving the party

B is certainly going to find it easier to let their hair down. What else about the handwriting points to this?

Next time you are feeling angry or agitated, try repeating this pattern with your normal pen or pencil.

Apparently, making this wave-like movement with your pen helps to release tension and stress (no guarantee, I'm afraid). Keep doing it

until you feel yourself calming down and then turn over the paper to check whether the pressure feels lighter.

If it's heavier then stop immediately, because it certainly isn't helping in the way it should!

Can you find samples of your handwriting written at various stages of your life that exert a variety of pressures? Has your handwriting pressure changed over the years? Can you think of any reason why that would be?

What does your handwriting pressure say about you?

Do you have heavy pressure?

YES

Is it *very heavy*?

YES → YOU SOMETIMES FIND IT HARD NOT TO LOSE YOUR TEMPER

NO → YOU ARE LIKELY TO BE A LEADER AND CAN BE ASSERTIVE

Do you have 'pasty' handwriting?

YES → YOU ARE SUPER SENSUAL!

NO

Is it 'normal'?

YES → YOU HAVE HEALTHY RESPONSES TO STRESS

Is it light?

YES → YOU ARE SENSITIVE AND CAUTIOUS

Do you have 'sharp' handwriting?

YES → YOU ARE SENSITIVE AND SAVE YOUR PHYSICAL ENERGY FOR WHEN IT'S NEEDED

WHOSE LINE IS IT ANYWAY?

Look at these two handwritings.

Sigmund Freud

Benjamin Britten

As you can see, Sigmund Freud has the heavier pressure. What does this say about him, and what other aspects of the handwriting that you have learned so far back this up?

What can you tell about Benjamin Britten?

Sigmund Freud

Freud's handwriting shows pasty strokes with a marked right slant. He has also found it hard to avoid tangling of the lines.

As I hope you can detect in his handwriting, Freud was not frightened of speaking his mind – in fact he often found it difficult to remain quiet!

The breadth and depth of his writing shows strong creativity, sensuality and a whole lot of charm. The tall, straight strokes and the strong right slant indicate communication skills and a keen intellect, but that tangling does show that sometimes he could get carried away and a bit muddled. Judging from this writing, do you think he was likely to back down in an argument?

Benjamin Britten

Benjamin Britten has a much more regular, well-spaced and lighter handwriting. Look at those steady baselines – the composer had composure!

He shows refinement and, like Freud, once again high intelligence, but unlike Freud he must have been happy with his own company – that small middle zone points to a pared-down ego.

When you have finished reading my book and have gained a little more knowledge, come back to this sample and see if you can find other clues that would help you imagine what Sigmund Freud would have made of Benjamin Britten if he had been one of his patients.

Chapter 7

SIZE

Size matters.

Even without knowing anything about graphology, we can make assumptions about a person's character from the size of their letters and words. Most people would agree that a large handwriting denotes an extrovert and larger-than-life individual.

Some people write large all the time and others only do so according to their transient mood.

One very important factor to take into consideration before analysis is the size of the piece of paper, notebook or postcard that is being written on. If you have large, extravagant writing you may need to shrink it a little or a lot to fit your words on a postcard. Therefore the easiest way of judging this aspect of handwriting is from an average-sized letter paper or A4-sized sheet.

The blank piece of paper represents the person's environment or 'world', and the way in which they occupy that space will tell us a lot about the writer. The size of writing is indicative of how much of that world we choose to take up.

How extrovert are you? Do you crave company or are you happy to be on your own?

Whether you fill your environment to the edges or feel happier to keep yourself under the radar – all is about to be revealed.

Average Size

I feel fairly average.

To get a clear idea of sizing, always judge the overall size by the size of the middle zone, and refer back to Chapter 3 if necessary.

This average-sized writer has a balanced view towards sociability and is neither a screaming extrovert nor a shrinking violet.

I feel fairly average

Large Size

I love to party!

If the handwriting looks larger than the average then you are likely to be looking at someone who is outgoing, has no problem meeting new people and may even really enjoy putting themselves into the public eye.

They may not be so good at concentrating for hours on end because they have a need to go out and make their mark on the world. However, they can be great planners too, because they aren't put off by a seemingly overwhelming project.

Very Large Size

look at me!

Just occasionally you will come across a handwriting that literally demands attention because the letters seem to bounce off the page due to their size and boldness.

The page will look crammed and there is little room on the page for anything else other than the writer and their ego.

This personality is impatient to be seen as not only sociable but also ambitious and successful. Concentration is unlikely to be good because they have an insatiable hunger for attention and can be exhausting to be around. They might be boastful, undisciplined and easily distracted.

As ever, do look at this in context. Look out for other signs that the writer may be concealing feelings of inadequacy; by the end of the book you will have enough knowledge to spot the mixed signals that point to a less than confident individual.

Small Size

I'm not that sociable

Many people think that small handwriting is the sign of an introverted personality, but I like to think that it indicates people who are happy in their own company. They are not necessarily crippled with shyness. Their concentration is likely to be good, and they will be economical with their displays of emotion as well as in all areas of their life, but it won't necessarily mean they are insecure.

If their writing is not overly small but merely a little smaller than average then the writer may very well have normal feelings of sociability while possessing a high degree of independence. There may be other signs of strong willpower and determination that can propel them to the top of their career ladder faster than their less modest friends and colleagues.

Very Small Size

I'd rather be left alone

Is the handwriting so small that you could almost describe it as microscopic?

If so, it's safe to assume that this writer is very deep into their own life and thoughts, and gives little time or space to others. Although powers of concentration can still be good, this intensely introverted individual is a deep thinker, but there can also be signs of depression, especially if the writer doesn't consistently write this small.

Uneven Size

Can't quite Make Up my Mind.

If there is an unusually wide range of sizes, particularly in the middle zone, then this points to an individual who is unfocused, inconsistent in their need to communicate with others and seemingly moody.

This type of person can be quite selfish, as they tend not to realise or want to accept that their behaviour can leave others feeling perplexed.

A little variation in size is quite normal, but a wide variety and on a consistent basis points to some instability similar to a very inconsistent slant, as we saw in Chapter 5.

Larger or smaller words or letters

A *I really love him*

B *Not sure I like him much*

C *Good luck with it all*

Sometimes your eye will be drawn to a word or an individual letter on the page that sticks out because the size is different from the rest of the text.

A. I think this person really does LOVE him!

B. We can be certain that he or she doesn't like him much at all.

C. A big 'k' is associated with a rather defiant and stubborn individual.

Have a look carefully at the word in question and try to remember what you've learned from previous examples of words that don't fit in with the rest of the text.

Exercise 9: Size

Have a good look at your own handwriting: how would you judge the overall size and what does this say about you, do you think?

Can you understand now why a higher than average number of mathematicians, musicians and scientists have a small-sized writing as opposed to actors, PR executives and politicians, who exhibit a generally larger style?

Who out of these two appears to be the more composed?

A   *Please can I borrow your lovely hat?*

B   *Please can I borrow your lovely hat?*

The answer is B. Not only is the size average, but it is also fairly stable without huge variations. This person is also more likely than A to actually return the hat to the owner in its original condition.

What do you think it means if the personal pronoun (I) is much larger than the rest of the script?

I'm Currently in a great job

As opposed to this less self-obsessed writer:

Then i said to them
' let's go'.

All will be revealed in Chapter 14, when we discuss personal pronouns in detail.

Try writing double the size of your normal writing and then, with the same sentence, reduce your handwriting to about half the size that you are used to. How does this make you feel, and which of the two feels more comfortable?

Make a note of how your writing changes. This experiment should have made your handwriting slow right down as you write in a way that is unnatural to you.

Find samples of writing that you wrote when you were forced to concentrate intently: you are likely to see that the size becomes smaller as your concentration increases or larger as you lose concentration. This pattern is often seen in children's writing.

What do you think happened to this writer to make them suddenly increase the size of their writing at the end of the script?

Dear Sir,

I would like to be considered for the position of accountant at your company.

I am well qualified and can supply excellent references.

Yours faithfully
Jill Smith

It is likely that Jill simply lost concentration towards the end of the letter and her attention span didn't stretch to finish it.

Would you employ her as an accountant?

What does the _size_ of your handwriting say about you?

Do you have a
'normal' writing size?

YES

Is the size consistent?

YES

YOU HAVE A HEALTHY
VIEW OF SOCIALISING
AND ARE HAPPY TO BE
ALONE WHEN NECESSARY

NO

THE VARIATION OF
SIZE COULD POINT
TO RESTLESSNESS

TAKE NOTE OF
INDIVIDUAL WORDS
AFFECTED

NO

Is it large?

YES

YOU ENJOY
BEING WITH
OTHERS AND
ARE EXTROVERT

Is it very
large?

YES

WATCH OUT
FOR SELF-
CENTREDNESS!

NO

Is it small?

YES

YOU HAVE GOOD
CONCENTRATION AND
CAN WORK ALONE

Is it very
small?

YES

YOU SHOW INDICATIONS
OF EXTREME INTROVERSION
AND MAY BE PRONE TO
EXCESSIVE ANXIETY

WHOSE LINE IS IT ANYWAY?

What can you make of these two rather different individuals?

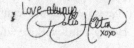

Paris Hilton

Sir Isaac Newton

Paris Hilton

Paris has a consistently large-sized writing which shows that she is not afraid to perform in front of her public. She is bold and is likely to enjoy the limelight. Her concentration may not be brilliant but the vertical slant indicates that she is able to keep her emotions in check and let her head rule her heart.

However, the upper-zone strokes are small compared to her middle zone and lower zone so this points to the intellect taking second place to her day-to-day activities and her interest in the material world, but she is much more cautious than perhaps her flamboyant signature may lead others to believe.

Sir Isaac Newton

This second sample of handwriting belongs to one of the most influential scientists of all time and his fantastic powers of concentration and attention to detail are shown in the small handwriting. There is evidence of a 'pasty' stroke, and by now you will have figured out that this may indicate an interest in the more sensual aspects of life (interestingly, he was reputed to have died a virgin).

Although Newton was clearly hard-working and gifted at school and university, it was during study and experimental work carried out on his own that he achieved his greatest discoveries, including the law of gravity.

Chapter 8

SPACING

The spacing in handwriting analysis refers to the distances between the individual letters, words, lines, as well as the space around the page (otherwise known as margins).

We have just looked at size of handwriting and how much space the writer takes up in his 'world'. In a similar way, the space that the writer subconsciously doesn't fill in gives us a really good indication of how they feel towards other people, about their social behaviour and also about their thinking patterns.

As I keep telling people who impress upon me that their handwriting is messy or downright illegible, the aesthetics of a writing are not likely to impress me as much as the actual mechanics of the writing. After all, calligraphy is quite a different skill from graphology!

However, there is no doubt that uneven or very cramped spacing makes for a confusing and muddled script. If an otherwise healthy writer shows a cramped, tightly spaced and illegible hand then it is quite clear that organisation skills are lacking.

On the other hand, a well-presented, well-spaced handwritten letter would point to an individual who can plan, think and act in a way that makes communication with others easier, and is likely to result in considered and rational thinking patterns.

I am normal because the spacing is just fine!

Once again we are forced to think about what is 'normal'. In this instance, normal refers to anything that is not abnormal! If the spacing does not tire you out with its tightly overlapping letters or lines and if it doesn't confuse you with oversized gaps and wide spaces between letters and huge open-plan margins, then you are probably looking at something that can be considered 'normal' or at least average.

How dare you say I'm not like other people!

Normal spacing is something we learn to develop as we begin to write and become more adept with a pencil or pen, and so do remember that young children, or those with poor literacy skills, may not yet have learned these skills and should not be judged by the same criteria.

SPACING BETWEEN WORDS

If we think about each word being the self or the ego, then we can equate the space left between words to how the writer positions him or herself with regard to society, not only emotionally but also sometimes physically.

Therefore normal well-spaced words on the page that look as though they are in harmony with each other show an intelligent and well-balanced individual – definitely someone who can deal with others and has a flexibility that makes them socially well adjusted.

Come round to my house any time

Small Space Between Words

Stand a little closer to me please.

Have you ever met someone who just doesn't understand about physical boundaries and perhaps backs you up against the wall at a party? Well, this individual may very well be the person who has just written the sentence above.

They may be overly touchy-feely, with a need for constant physical reassurance, but they may also be just plain intrusive and wanting to know everything about you on a first meeting.

They often display selfishness, perhaps because they never stop talking and smothering would be the end result . . . not a great trait!

Large Space Between Words

I'm   happiest   when   I'm   alone   so   go   now.

Not surprisingly, this writer's issue is that they tend to put up barriers between themselves and others. They are extremely hard to get to know and they may have justifiably earned the reputation of being a bit of an enigma.

They always value their privacy and others may find it hard to communicate with them, other than perhaps via a written note slid under a locked door.

SPACING BETWEEN LETTERS

The space between the letters themselves gives us a better understanding of how the writer relates to individuals as opposed to society as a whole.

I have always seen the space between letters as a reflection of the writer's social comfort zone and another indication of either introversion or extroversion.

Small Space Between Letters

Im like a coiled spring

This just looks pent up, doesn't it? Well, the writer certainly is! You can be sure that they are as narrow-minded as their writing, continually tense and not the sort of person other people will feel they can open up to.

Large Space Between Letters

Hi there - welcome !

This person is certainly more extrovert and more outgoing, but could be considered a little intrusive if the spaces are extremely wide. It shows that they simply don't know when to rein it in.

SPACING BETWEEN LINES

Spacing between lines shows us how the writer organises their thoughts, and once again how they express themselves within their environment.

Narrow Space Between Lines

Yesterday I moved the lawn, and did the housework and then took the dog for a walk.

This is so jumbled and cramped that it is difficult to read. Certainly communicative, the writer may actually be quite creative, but their thoughts are jumbled and they are unlikely to achieve as much as their imagination would like to.

They're not lacking in charm, but their excitability and liveliness can be exhausting.

Large Space Between Lines

I'm not sure I trust them to work for me - in fact

I'm better than them in

every way.

This person finds it hard to trust others and can quickly find themselves isolated either physically, emotionally or both. Extreme spacing could point to paranoia or snobbery. Either way, they choose to distance themselves.

MARGINS

The margins that we subconsciously leave around a piece of paper represent the 'frame' around the text.

Try to imagine the left margin as the past and the right margin as the future. This can be very revealing as to the writer's view towards professional and personal goals in life, cultural and artistic temperament, as well as his or her self-esteem levels. Now let's take a closer look . . .

The Well-Balanced Margins

I'm careful who I mix
with but I act with
poise and control. It is
interesting when you
come across unusual
characters but you need
to know how to act
in every situation. Do
you ever stop to think
about why everyone does
different things, it's a

This writer is, as you may have guessed, well balanced and enjoys a certain order to their life without being overly controlled.

Wide Left Margin

> I'd rather forget about what happened in the past because all of the things that come up with it can be troubling and lead me into thinking about things that I don't like to very often. It's a shame that it can be

As the left margin is what we are leaving behind and represents the past, we can safely say that this writer would rather move on quickly, forget what has happened and is eager to experience new situations and people. They can be extremely bold and brave, but if the left margin seems to be huge compared to the right then there is a real avoidance of any issue connected to the past.

Narrowing Left Margin

> I'm so tired because I have a lot to do and I really want to get it all done. It's difficult to concentrate when you feel so exhausted but it is very important to finish everything before tomorrow. If I don't I could get myself in trouble and have even more to worry about...

This writer finds it hard to move on from the past and wears themselves out with worry, which could lead to depression.

Widening Left Margin

Here we see someone who is increasingly impatient to crack on with their life, or at least that is how they feel at the time of writing. They tend to have an optimistic, even happy-go-lucky attitude.

Uneven Left Margin

This is the rebel, the writer who preserves their independence and perhaps possesses a stubborn streak because they simply don't like adhering to rules.

Wide Right Margin

If you remember that the right-hand margin represents the future, then you can be sure that this writer is fearful of the unknown, a little timid perhaps, and is unlikely to be the first to suggest bungee jumping for fun.

Narrowing Right Margin

A narrowing right margin could be due to poor organisational abilities – they haven't left enough room for the words – or it can be a positive sign in that the writer is relaxing into what they are writing, and feeling more comfortable.

Widening Right Margin

Unlike the narrowing right margin, this shows someone who is visibly becoming increasingly fearful and is finding the subject matter difficult to approach.

Uneven Right Margin

This is a writer with somewhat erratic thoughts and feelings. Not someone you want around in a crisis!

Wide Upper Margin

It is quite normal to have a wide upper margin at the beginning of a letter, particularly if you include an address and date at the top, but if every page has a wide upper space then the writer feels a need for formality with everyone. They may be even a little in awe or fear of others.

Narrow Upper Margin

Here we can observe a lack of formality, or perhaps a lack of respect.

Wide Lower Margin

In my experience the wide lower margin is usually made by someone who is trying to make it look as though they have written more than they actually have – an illusion of generosity. However, some graphologists see this trait as one of reserve or even aloofness.

Narrow Lower Margin

This could be another illusion – a desire to communicate for the sake of it. It is also indicative of someone who is rather greedy and materialistic.

No Margins

There has been no space left around the page and the writing looks overwhelming and even a little 'in your face'. This writer is pretty much the same when you meet them.

There are few boundaries that they are aware of and they will fill every available space in conversation with their chatter!

Wide Margins All Round

These writers tend to possess artistic sensitivities and in particular have a great sense of colour and form.

They may not be the most sociable, but refinement is important to them.

With all the various ways in which we use up the space on the paper, there are also various combinations of spacing that have interesting connotations. Let's explore a bit deeper . . .

Wide Letters Spaced Far Apart

save me a place

Having wide letters spaced far apart is an indication of an extrovert. Have a look at the overall size of the writing as well. Make sure that the spaces between the words aren't too wide though . . .

Narrow Letters With Narrow Spaces Between Words

Please don't leave me

This kind of person needs to be around others. Often fearful of life, they can get bogged down by worry; their need for emotional and physical support can be suffocating.

Narrow Letters With Wide Spaces Between Letters and Words

yes of course I'd love to

Don't be fooled by this writer – they can appear to be outgoing and sociable but deep down they are fraught with anxiety, and it is difficult for them to relax.

Irregular Letter Spacing

Honestly I'd love to see

Moody and difficult to fathom, this writer just can't work out what they want. In particular they may well have trouble in sustaining relationships due to their changing attitudes.

Irregular Word Spacing

Why don't people listen to me?

Not only does irregular word spacing point to someone who is fairly disorganised, as I mentioned at the beginning of this chapter, but it also betrays someone's inability to stop talking, often at the expense of listening to anyone else.

Irregular Line Spacing

Tell me all about how you
got on the other day?
Was it fun? Did you

see your friends? Tomorrow
I'm going to see

Irregular gaps between lines is another indication of rather unfocused thought patterns and muddled thinking. Planning and organisation is likely to be compromised.

Unconscious Columns of Space or 'Rivers'

Dear Sir,
Thank you for your letter.
It was a pleasure to
see you and I would
love to see you again
next week.

This quirk is often seen alongside wide spacing between words and is indicative of a person who feels vulnerable and has a subconscious desire to keep in control of their emotions, but also to control the environment and other people around them.

Exercise 10: Spacing

Jot down what you can judge about the spacing within your own 'Real You' sample. What does it say about you and the way you interact with the world around you?

Have a look at these examples and see if you can answer the questions below.

A *Hello how are you?*

B *Hello how are you?*

C *Hello howare you!*

D *Hello how are you?*

1 **Who is the most relaxed?**

2 **Who is narrow-minded and a bit uptight?**

3 **Who needs help unravelling their feelings?**

Answers

1) A. This writer is relaxed, but how sociable are they?

2) D. What does the small size indicate?

3) C. Do you think the exclamation mark could be compensation for something?

What does your _letter spacing_ say about you?

Are the spaces between letters wide?

 YES

 NO

YOU ARE LIKELY TO
BE OUTGOING

YOU MAY FIND IT
DIFFICULT TO LET
YOUR HAIR DOWN

Is your word spacing wide too?

Do you have narrow spaces between words?

YES

NO

YES

NO

YOU HAVE A STRONG
NEED FOR ATTENTION
BUT CLOSER
FRIENDSHIPS MAY BE
HARDER TO FIND

YOU ARE
SOCIALLY
WELL ADAPTED

YOU ARE A LITTLE
INHIBITED AND
UPTIGHT BUT LIKE
THE COMPANY
OF OTHERS

YOU ARE SOCIABLE
WITHOUT CROWDING
OTHERS

What does your word spacing say about you?

Is your word spacing wide?

YES →
YOU ARE INDEPENDENT AND CAN WORK ON YOUR OWN

Is the spacing very wide?

YES →
THERE MAY BE SOME ISOLATION FROM SOCIETY

NO →
YOU ARE HAPPY WITH YOUR OWN COMPANY

NO →
Is it average / normal?

YES →
YOU ARE WELL ORGANISED AND INTELLIGENT

NO →
Is it very narrow?

YES →
YOU HAVE A STRONG NEED TO BE WITH OTHERS

NO →
YOU ARE FRIENDLY BUT NOT NEEDY

What does your line spacing say about you?

Is your line spacing normal?

YES

YOU ARE FLEXIBLE
AND HAVE A GOOD
ORGANISATIONAL ABILITY

NO

Is it wide?

YES

YOU MAY FEAR
CLOSENESS AND
MAY BE A LITTLE
SUSPICIOUS
OF OTHERS.
YOU MAY ALSO
BE EXTRAVAGANT!

NO

Is it narrow?

YES

YOU ARE LIVELY AND
FUN BUT NOT WELL
ORGANISED.

NO

Is it irregular?

YES

ARE YOU MOODY?

WHOSE LINE IS IT ANYWAY?

Have a look at the sample writings of the well-known characters below and try and work out what their spacing says about them.

both pray that thing will get easier for you.

Prince William

thanks for the copy which
you have kindly sent me.
Yours very sincerely
Joseph Lister

Joseph Lister

I'm so happy that you are
here. This will be
FUN. Jimmy

Jimmy Fallon

It was exhilerating, intelligent,
inspiring. I now want to dance,
"become a part of the music — be in
the eye — and experience a moment
of monumental stillness."
Wow! Thank you. Oprah Winfrey

Oprah Winfrey

WAYS OF FEELING... I DO
BELIEVE THAT PAINTING
CAN CHANGE THE WORLD"
DAVID HOCKNEY

David Hockney

and liberalism which I set
to defend, I ask you to
give me the effective
vote and influence.
Yours faithfully,
Winston Churchill

Winston Churchill

Prince William

Prince William's writing consists of narrow letters but relatively wide spaces between words.

This future King of England will be more than a little used to socialising and meeting an extremely broad range of people. However, we can see that he is quite shy in reality and would not normally choose to push himself forward or hog the limelight. The wide spaces between his words show his need for some independence and privacy.

Joseph Lister

The nineteenth-century British surgeon's writing has well-spaced letters and words as well as a regular and quite broad line spacing.

Lister was certainly refined, with a clarity of purpose and a cautious approach to life. In fact, the spacing is so regular that it points towards a man of enormous self-control. The margins are by comparison quite narrow, which means that he may also have been rather self-centred.

Jimmy Fallon

Jimmy shows wide spacing all round which indicates that he loves attention but is also able to spend time on his own.

From what you have learned so far, what else can you tell about him? Look at the baseline, the tall upper zones . . .

Oprah Winfrey

This person is another TV great. Look at the tangled lines and the narrow spaces between the letters.

Oprah has a huge and lively personality but she can often feel overwhelmed with emotions. There are a lot of other interesting things to note about her handwriting: tightly closed and knotted ovals, middle zone going into the lower zone, the falling off of lines at the end of the page. Can you make your own interpretation of these things?

David Hockney

Another big character here – David Hockney has chosen to print and not use cursive writing but his spacing is pretty tightly knit on all fronts.

A true creative, he has a strong need to express himself and enjoys inter-action with others. Despite the narrow spacing between lines, he avoids tangling, which in itself shows that he is able to forge his own unique path without losing himself to poor organisation and chaos.

Winston Churchill

This famous wartime prime minister and statesman shows wide letter spacing and narrow letters but fairly wide spacing between the words themselves.

Winston Churchill was able to reach out to people, was sociable but also very much protected his independence and liked to do his own thing. Do you think this writing shows evidence of a broad pen stroke? – note that some of the smaller letters are ink-filled. What do you think this means? Refer back to Chapter 6, when we discussed 'pasty' writing.

Chapter 9

SPEED

When we first learn to write, the speed of our handwriting is slow as we are learning to form letters. In our subsequent school years, we are encouraged to keep our handwriting legible and so a speedy scrawl is not appropriate or acceptable.

However, as we grow older and we develop our own handwriting style and develop our own pace of life, some of us will speed things up while others will remain more precise and slow.

As with all things, a balancing act is required to achieve the best results – too speedy and the writing becomes illegible and letters are poorly formed, if at all. This may point to an impatient and careless individual.

If our writing is too slow and deliberate, or with letter formations retraced, then the graphological analysis may not be that complimentary either as it may indicate someone who rather overthinks their actions and their words. They may be lacking in spontaneity.

Speed is an important part of high form quality, which we will explore in a later chapter, but a reasonably good quality of form is an indication of speedy thought processes and mental agility. Therefore in a slow handwriting we can make the assumption that the writer is more calculating and certainly more self-conscious.

A writer who is slow of thought and action may not be as quick-witted as their speedier counterpart. It can also be indicative of a calculating, even dishonest nature.

Stress can also affect speed quite significantly and, depending on the individual, can cause them to slow down or speed up. So, as ever, be vigilant concerning variations when looking at multiple handwriting samples from the same person before drawing any definite conclusions.

There are other reasons why writers may have an unusually slow writing speed: dyslexics may write more slowly than non-dyslexics, as may writers with physical disabilities. Under these circumstances it is, of course, not wise to judge on speed.

Generally, the speed of the writing reflects the writer's vital force. It is a good yardstick for assessing intelligence and energy levels.

Another factor to consider is the spontaneity of the writer: is he or she writing under duress? What is their relationship with the intended recipient? Perhaps they are writing notes for themselves, in which case there is likely to be less hesitation.

A shopping list to one's self may not be written at the same speed as a Dear John letter . . .

It doesn't matter who you are writing to: if you are a naturally speedy writer then slowing your handwriting right down is going to feel just plain unnatural. The opposite is true if you are a slow writer suddenly turbo-charging your handwriting.

There are signs you can look for to see if someone has been writing a message slowly or quickly.

Slow Traits

Here are some obvious clues:

Disconnected letters within words – each time we take the pen or pencil off the page we are slowing our speed.

Heavy pressure – the added pressure and stress in heavy writing takes more effort and time.

Retraced stroke – going over a stroke that you have already written slows the speed.

Embellishment – complicated strokes, curlicues or unnecessary flourishes slow everything down.

Falling baseline – the natural flow of handwriting will be horizontal or gently rising from a speedier hand (see Chapter 4 on baselines).

Angled or arcaded forms of connection (see Chapter 10) – these strokes are much slower to create than garlands or threads.

Carefully placed or leftward placed 'i' dots and 't' bars – a really speedy hand may miss these out altogether, or at least the natural direction of the hand would tend to place them to the right of the stem.

Leftward slant – as we saw in Chapter 5, a left slant goes against the natural rhythm of moving forward.

Extremely concise and regular letter forms that mimic the copy-book style taught at school – a speedy hand will have developed a unique style that is likely to include a type of short form, moving away from the copybook but still legible.

Large spaces between words – just leaving those gaps takes precious nanoseconds.

There is nothing the matter with taking your time...

Can you see how many slow factors are in the writing sample above?

A handwriting or forensic expert looking for signs of a forgery would also look for signs of a slow script. At first glance, signatures could be identical but to an expert there would be 'tells' relating to slower speed or hesitation – the biro or pen tends to make darker marks and dots when pausing.

Forgery is a highly specialised field – do leave it to the experts – but you can look for breaks in letters, dots and pause marks.

I'd just like to say that
It was a delight to
See   you   .

Fast Traits

Below is a list of identifiable signs:

Rising baseline – as the name suggests, this is a naturally rising baseline.

Regularity – does the writing look regular, without any huge changes in size, spacing, etc.?

Connected – if the letters are connected then the writer hasn't wasted time lifting pen from paper.

Light to normal pressure – the lighter the pressure, the speedier the writing.

Left margin that widens – the writer is so keen to get finished that the margin gets wider and wider.

A consistent right slant – if the slant is facing the direction that allows it to move forward easily, then you can be sure that this is a speedy hand.

'i' dots and 't' bars to the right – much quicker to dot and cross to the right rather than backtracking.

End strokes that go to the right – as in the sample below.

Hi there, see you soon

Simplified letter formations – are the 'o's and 'a's not closed, or perhaps the writer has adopted speedy short forms?

What's happening? Look me up soon!

So we have ascertained that, generally speaking, a fast speed equates to a fast mind, which is often associated with a higher IQ and intelligence.

However, we can all feel self-conscious when we are talking or communicating with people we don't know particularly well, or especially when we feel a need to make an impression. Therefore our speed can certainly change when we are pushed out of our comfort zone socially or emotionally. But what about when we are actually lying? A sudden change in speed can indicate that the writer has had to 'stop and think' because something does not come naturally to him or her.

Exercise 11: Speed

Are you a slow but steady tortoise, or a boy racer? Tick off how many slow and how many fast traits you have in your own handwriting. What is your overall speed? Do the same test on your nearest and dearest and then deduce who is first to reach the finish line . . .

Which of these writers is the more patient and meticulous?

A *Rushing to get things done*

B *Rushing to get things done*

The answer is A. B may be more spontaneous and creative but also more likely to make a mistake.

This writer has speedy writing but what other traits can you see and what do you think this may mean?

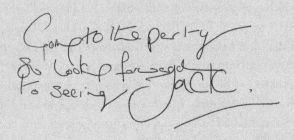

Answer: This script is definitely speedy with the short forms, ill-formed letters and 'i' and 't' dots and bars to the right. There is narrow spacing between both words and lines which make the writing look messy and cramped. This shows that the writer hates to be alone and tends to crowd others. There is likely to be a lack of constructive planning.

The overall size is large, which adds to the extroversion of the writer, but there is a variety of lower-zone endings which point to physical restlessness and perhaps a need to have a varied physical life. The word 'Jack' is so prominent, though, that for the time being at least he appears to literally take up a big part of their thinking!

What does your handwriting speed say about you?

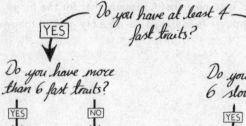

Do you have at least 4 fast traits?

YES

Do you have more than 6 fast traits?

YES

ALTHOUGH YOU HAVE A QUICK MIND YOU ARE PRONE TO MAKING CARELESS MISTAKES AND YOU CAN BE IMPATIENT

NO

YOU ARE QUICK-WITTED, SPONTANEOUS AND HAVE A GENERALLY UPBEAT ATTITUDE TO LIFE

NO

Do you have more than 6 slow traits?

YES

YOU CAN BE VERY SELF-CONSCIOUS, HATE SURPRISES AND YOU CAN FIND IT HARD TO GRASP ABSTRACT CONCEPTS

OR ARE YOU A MASTER CRIMINAL? - JUST KIDDING!

NO

YOU ARE CAUTIOUS, CAN BE METICULOUS AND FEEL HAPPIER AMONGST MORE PREDICTABLE AND LESS VOLATILE PEOPLE

ARE YOU AN ACCOUNTANT? - JUST SAYING...

WHOSE LINE IS IT ANYWAY?

Here are two different speedy writing samples. Can you list the traits that suggest a fast writing and what is the difference between them?

no photographers to lend out. I usually let the studio send out stills for the latest film. But I want you to know I appreciate your letter and kind words! Best wishes

meryl streep

Thankyou for your message of congratulation following the General Election. I did appreciate it.

With every good wish.

Margaret Thatcher

Meryl Streep

Margaret Thatcher

Here is an example of a much slower speed. Why do I say that and what does this say about them?

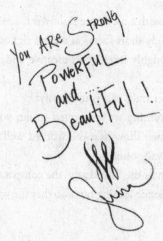

Serena Williams

Meryl Streep

This doyenne of Hollywood has many fast traits, including strong connection of letters, a rightward slant and a rightward stroke that ends her signature.

Ms Streep is intelligent, witty, knows her own mind and is keen to look to the future.

What other handwriting traits can you identify as well as the speed? Look at the baseline – it is flexible. She has plenty of energy, is a little moody at times, but always exciting!

The narrow line spacing points to a lively and expressive demeanour.

The loops on the upper and lower zone show that she possesses both a strong imagination and a certain restlessness.

Margaret Thatcher

Whatever your political leanings, there is no doubt that the late Lady Thatcher had a speedy handwriting.

The writing is regular, with a moderate right slant, straight – but not overly so – baselines, many speedy short forms as well as rightward 't' bars.

The writing shows a highly intelligent, creative and, at times, impatient writer.

Once again, what other traits can you identify?

If you remember everything we've covered so far, you'll notice the wide word and line space, which show that she worked well on her own and, in fact, needed her own privacy often.

Despite her reputation as the 'Iron Lady' the comparatively small middle-zone letters show an academic leaning but also that she was not driven by ego.

Serena Williams

This tennis star certainly excels on the court and her handwriting is also very distinctive, but it has a slow speed. How can we tell this?

Serena has disconnected her letters for the most part, with the exception of her signature. The size of the writing is large but it is also irregular in that there are non-capital letters such as the 's' in 'strong' and the 'f' and 'l' in 'powerful' and 'beautiful', which are particularly large, and written in capitals.

The slant is vertical except for a left-slanted signature.

Serena enjoys the limelight and is certainly no shrinking violet, either on the court or off it. However, she is extremely cautious in her dealings with others, and is a meticulous planner.

What else have you learned about Serena, based on all your new-found knowledge?

She is instinctive and intuitive, and the lack of loops in her long lower-zone strokes means that she is likely to call a spade a spade (or perhaps a racquet a racquet).

The left slant to her signature might cause you to wonder whether her feelings about herself don't always match her extrovert and confident public persona.

Compare your own handwriting to Serena's. How do you think you two would get on? Game, set and match? Or double fault?

Chapter 10

CONNECTING STROKES AND SHAPES

In the previous chapters we have touched upon spacing, size and speed. We've also taken into account the way letters connect within a word. Here we're going to focus on the shape of the strokes of the connections in more detail.

Some connections are speedy, feel natural and fluid to make, and will take the line of least resistance. Certainly, in most copybook styles, this is how we are taught to write. These connections are called '**garlands**' and look like this . . .

Garland

write well

Sometimes the line of least resistance takes on new meaning when the connecting strokes become so unformed they are almost like straight lines. This is called 'thread'.

Thread

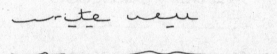

Harder work and more time consuming is the 'arcade' connection. You can see why these connecting strokes are called arcade from the patterns in the example below.

Arcade

The final connecting stroke is rather spiky and, funnily enough, is referred to as an 'angle'.

Angle

When you start to look at handwriting to assess the connecting stroke, also look at the way the writer has written the letters 'm' and 'n' because the shape of these letters will often imitate the shape of the connecting strokes:

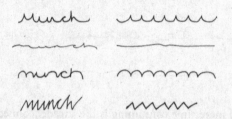

The four different 'munch's have been rather stylised for effect but it will help you to understand the variances between the different shapes.

So, the letters 'm' and 'n' and the connecting strokes are what we are looking at, but what does it all mean, and what if we have an amalgamation of garlands, threads, arcades and angles in our handwriting?

In fact, most of us have a combination of all four, but there is likely to be one connecting stroke that takes precedence over the others. If you do come across a 'pure' angle thread, arcade or garland connector, then it may be that the writer is not so well balanced, but rather extreme, depending on the shape they use.

Let's take a good look at each of the four main shapes and their subsections.

The Garland Formation

The garland uses an underhand, concave movement and looks a bit like a cup or an open vessel. It usually indicates a receptive, easy-going and open personality.

These writers tend to be emotionally expressive but non-combative and, in fact, would rather avoid conflict altogether. They look for security in life and favour convention and routine. Most people would find them kind if a little uncomplicated. In the work environment they are most likely to be flexible and adaptable, and show compassion to others.

How can I help you?

SHALLOW GARLAND

just do what you want

This writer is using a garland shape but it looks rather lazy, doesn't it? The curves are indeed shallow and made with minimum effort.

These writers are still kind, especially on a superficial level, and can appear extremely willing to help and show sympathy. But in a work or personal relationship, it can soon become obvious that they are passive partners.

They will contribute when asked, but feelings may not have much depth to them and hasty indifference follows initial enthusiasm. This could manifest as complacency, thoughtlessness or even selfishness.

SHAM GARLAND

These are garlands but not as we know them. Look out for excessive retracing, while the 'm's and 'n's look like waves in the sea!

manipulative

These people can be manipulative, using kindness and charm not to benefit others, but to help them get what and where they want. Unfortunately, they are often very bright and climb the ladder of success using cunning over aggression. They are not averse to the odd untruth. We've all met people like that, haven't we?

THE CLOTHES LINE GARLAND

look how good I am

It's easy to get this shape confused with the shallow garland, but look for garland shapes that are dragged out a bit too long with a wider space between the letters to accommodate.

Here is the writer who knows just how wonderful they are and are keen that others should know it too.

THE DROOPY GARLAND

If you are as old as me you may remember that at one point curtains which resembled old droopy knickers hanging over the windows were deemed fashionable. What *were* we thinking?

it's a great burden

This is an interesting personality. Just by looking at the writing above, you may be beginning to feel guilty. If so then this is exactly what the writer intended. These people are rather wonderfully skilled at being martyrs. They will do anything to help, even though they're already burdened down with the stresses and strains of life. And they won't let you forget it.

So, as you can see, garlands are not all equal – they can be tolerant, kind, sociable, sympathetic but also lazy, deceptive and manipulative.

The Thread Formation

Look at that squiggly line and at the unformed, thready connecting shapes. I love, love, love these people (there's a reason for this: I'm a threader myself).

As with other connecting shapes, there are positive and negative sides to this personality.

These people tend to be quick-witted but can also be careless and in too much of a hurry to finish a project.

Why are they rushing and what is the illegibility covering up? The absence of angles can mean that they don't like conflict and there is likely to be a strong diplomatic streak in their DNA. But the excessive threading and illegibility could also mean that they avoid the painful truth by literally covering up their communication route.

In the same way that a child will avoid telling the truth if caught red-handed by changing the subject or distracting an adult with a cover story, the thready writer may be 'glossing' over elements of his or her personality.

Thready, indistinct writing can also be a sign of tiredness or just transitory unhappiness so, as always, do check that this is a regular and not occasional facet of the handwriting.

Let's look at the different sort of thread formations and connective strokes.

THE LEGIBLE SPEEDY THREAD

I had such fun today

This writer is intelligent and communicative and is likely to be creative. They dislike routine and convention. They are fun and spontaneous but will fight against any restrictions in life. They tend to be highly intuitive and curious about the world and the people in it.

Their powers of observation and ability to communicate make them excellent psychologists and graphologists. Naturally.

THE END-OF-WORD THREAD

fascinating though he ...

These people have a tendency to lead you up the garden path with what appears to be genuine interest, just before they fade away and disappear. Intelligent and diplomatic, they are often geniuses at extracting information about others but impenetrable to those who want to get closer to them.

THE MIDDLE-OF-WORD THREAD

I'm a trifle confused.

If he or she chooses to 'thread out' the middle of words, they can be blanking out or bypassing reality. They will avoid conflict through fear and overcaution.

These traits also point to someone who is rather unreliable, 'flaky' and inconsiderate. Like the end-of-word threaders, these people are difficult to read, hard to know and unlikely to open up to others.

This can be a great tragedy, because middle-of-word threading can also suggest a writer who doesn't always feel so great about themselves and would benefit from reaching out more.

THE INCONSISTENT THREAD

You may come across someone who has a perfectly legible, well-formed handwriting and then goes and executes the occasional and inconsistent thread that will catch your eye.

Let's talk about Michael and how he's getting on.

This could be the result of a lapse of concentration, but on the other hand it could betray a need to be ambiguous, evasive or concealing. Does this inconsistent threading happen often, or is it a genuine one-off?

If it is the latter, could there be a reason why a particular word or phrase has been glossed over?

The Arcade Formation

As we've already discussed, the arcade formation is a little more time-consuming to create and its convex, roof-like shape indicates a more cautious and self-protective character.

You may notice a certain aloofness or old-fashioned formality to the personality of the writer in question, which can be beguiling.

However, this style can also point to men and women who are emotionally controlled or even controlling. They certainly aren't easily influenced or dominated by others, and displays of emotion are likely to be reserved for trusted friends and family.

Do I know you?

THE PURE ARCADE

I'm not changing

When you see arcaded connection strokes without a combination of the others, then you are looking at a rather inflexible individual. They can be immensely hard-working and painstaking, but you can be sure they are only going to put themselves forward for the top position. In a nutshell, they consider themselves quite simply the boss.

THE OVERSIZED ARCADE

who am I?

Any exaggeration in the handwriting, as you already know, is often an overcompensation for a weakness of sorts. In this instance you have a show-off, hiding a fragile ego. Fine for the actor, magician, mime artist, but not so great for the bomb-disposal expert.

THE FLAT ARCADE

trust me

That canopy may be hiding a less-than-honest persona – they are creating a protective shell around them. Is this due to paranoia or dishonesty?

The Angle Formation

Straight talking

Angles can look a bit spiky, as they don't have the gentler curves associated with the other three styles above. This writer appears to take a direct route to the next letter, but with a rather determined and uncompromising attitude.

He or she is likely to be highly competitive, analytical and critical – both of themselves and sometimes of others.

However, they are determined and ambitious and can be very loyal to those they care about.

EXTREME ANGULARITY

just get out

Scared? You should be. If you see extreme angularity you will probably also see a heavier than average or very heavy pressure. Do refer back to Chapter 6.

Is the handwriting consistently like this or is it just a passing trait? Either way there is anger and hostility here, and these people will not take prisoners in seeking to get their own way in life. Inflexible and narrow-minded, this sort of attitude could spell health issues later in life unless they can learn to relax.

INCONSISTENT ANGULARITY

How are you?

Once again, have a look at the word or phrase that is highlighted with the unusual angle connections. If you know the writer then you can ask yourself if it has a particular resonance with the writer's character. If not, then this could just mean someone who has an erratic temper. Watch out!

Very few writers have 'pure' connective shapes, so let's have a look at a few common combinations:

Arcades and Angles

never go out

These writers are hard-working and good with detail, but they can lack a certain flexibility and find it difficult to establish an easy-going rapport with others.

Angles and Threads

lets just do it

Here we have the creativity of the thread writer combined with the go-getting action of the angle writer, which can be very positive indeed. On the other hand, this writer could be rather exhausting.

Garlands and Arcades

I love you deeply

This person is emotional and sociable, but has self-control too.

Garlands and Threads

or we could just do nothing at all

These writers can be charming but can also lack backbone and rigour. They may be a trifle lazy . . .

Garlands and Angles

ill help you

In this instance we have a healthy combination of practicality and emotion.

Arcades and Threads

wriggling out of

Here we have an interesting combination of double secrecy and creativity. Master of Illusion? Master criminal? An interesting one indeed . . .

Exercise 12: Connections

A *Hi there!*

B *hi there!*

C Hi there

D Hi there

Who is the most analytical?

The answer is A.

Who appears to be covering something up?

Both C and D are capable of deception.

Who would get creative in a hurry?

The answer is C.

Who is the most formal of these writers?

The answer is D.

Which one has the most in common with you?

Only you can answer this one! What style of connection do you have? Are you a 'pure' or a 'mixed' type?

Let's make it a bit harder . . .

Which one of these two plays the martyr?

A *I'u good*   B *I'm good*

Answer: B – look at those sham garlands. Don't they know it!

Who is the bigger show-off?

A *helllo*   B *hellllo*

Answer: Of course it's A: the big swooping arcades give the game away.

Which of these writers suffers from a low boredom threshold?

A *Happy Birthday*

B *Happy Birthday*

Answer: A – this thready writer just can't keep up their enthusiasm.

Which one of these writers is telling the truth about themselves?

A *I'm very tense*

B *I'm very tense*

Answer: Yes, of course, it's B. Although both writers show angularity it is only B that has that pure tense angular writing. And relax . . .

Now try writing out that same phrase yourself using all angles, even if that seems odd to you.

Has your pressure increased? Turn over the page and have a feel. It's really hard to write in an angular style without heavy pressure. What do you think that means?

Overleaf are some flow charts. Of course they are unlikely to all apply to the handwriting samples that you are looking at, so pick and choose the relevant ones.

What do your garland connections say about you?

Are your connecting strokes predominantly garland?

YES

NO → SEE OTHER FLOW CHARTS

Are they shallow?

YES → YOU CAN BE IMPULSIVE AND HASTY

NO → Are they deep or retraced?

YES → YOU ARE SYMPATHETIC AND DISLIKE DISCORD

Are they so retraced that they look like waves?

GUARD AGAINST TOO CUNNING A NATURE!

NO → Are the garlands regular and firm?

YES → YOU ARE DEMONSTRATIVE AND WARM

NO → IF YOU HAVE WEAK GARLANDS YOU MAY HAVE LOW ENERGY LEVELS

What do your _thread connections_ say about you?

Are your connecting strokes predominantly thread?

YES — NO

NO → SEE OTHER FLOW CHARTS!

Is your writing legible?

YES — NO

NO → YOU MAY BE INTELLIGENT BUT HAVE DIFFICULTY IN COMMUNICATING YOUR INTELLIGENCE!

Is threading at the ends of the words only?

YES — NO

YES → DIPLOMATIC AND A GOOD NEGOTIATOR BUT HARD TO FATHOM!

NO → YOU CAN SUFFER FROM INDECISION

Is threading inconsistent?

YES

YOU MAY BE VERY CREATIVE BUT A LITTLE ECCENTRIC!

What do your <u>arcade connections</u> say about you?

Are your connecting strokes predominantly arcade?

YES

YOU ARE TRADITIONAL
BY NATURE AND CAN
BE ARTISTIC

NO

SEE OTHER FLOW
CHARTS!

Are the arcades very big or extravagant?

YES

YOU MAY BE AN
ATTENTION SEEKER
OR DRAMATIST!

NO

Are they flat?

YES

YOU COULD BE
'COVERING UP' FOR
AN INSECURITY
OR FEAR...

What do your angle connections say about you?

Are your connecting strokes predominantly angle?

YES

NO → SEE OTHER FLOW CHARTS!

Do you have only angles as connecting strokes and 'M' and 'N' shapes also angles?

YES → YOU ARE DETERMINED, ANALYTICAL AND CRITICAL

ARE YOU DONALD TRUMP?

NO → Do you have angles and other secondary forms of connection?

YES → YOU ARE AN INTELLIGENT STRATEGIST BUT YOUR HEAD RULES YOUR HEART

WHOSE LINE IS IT ANYWAY?

Have a look at these famous handwritings and see if you can judge which predominant connecting stroke they use, and what that says about them.

Michelangelo

Kim Kardashian

Angelina Jolie

George Washington

Michelangelo

This text certainly looks formal and archaic compared to the loose, less stylised script that we prefer in modern times. However, there is an artistic precision in the regular angles that have been used in the occasional connecting stroke, but also in the 'm' and 'n' shapes.

This enormously famous artist had an eye for shape and form, as well as a strong, competitive and hard-working personality. If there were no other forms but angles in his writing then we could surmise that he was extremely uptight and rigid to the detriment of productivity. However, look at those occasional thready endings to words . . .

This combination denotes free-thinking creativity and open-minded curiosity that point to this person's genius.

Kim Kardashian

Kim has used a felt-tip pen to write her free-flowing signature. Her writing shows a variety of arcades and angles, and there are even thread endings as well!

This blend shows her to be perfectionist, hard-working and ambitious. Those thread endings make her diplomatic while giving her an edginess, which will come in handy when dealing with the press and adoring fans.

What do you think those long strokes from the middle to lower zone signify? If you can't remember, have a look back at Chapter 3, 'The Zones'.

Angelina Jolie

Angelina's handwriting is a great example of thready connection strokes as well as some flat arcades displayed in her 'm' and 'n' strokes.

It shows enormous creativity and sensitivity to others. This makes sense given what we know about her: someone who is broad-minded and curious, but far more reticent when it comes to her own life.

George Washington

George Washington's script presents a number of different connecting strokes. How many can you spot? The large number of arcades shows a good sense of proportion and a facility to mix with a wide variety of people. He was born to be in charge but he retains his own eccentricities.

The garland and thread formations indicate a quick mind, compassion and diplomacy. In summary, Washington was an extraordinary man of many talents.

Let's have a look at some more contemporary world leaders and see how their negotiating skills may differ, and whether they share any common ground.

Angela Merkel

Donald Trump

Vladimir Putin

Angela Merkel

The German leader's handwriting is an excellent example of deep, retraced garland connectors. She is contemplative, sedate and sympathetic but may find it hard to move on from relationships or situations.

Donald Trump

Wow, those angles look like a graph!

President Trump is analytical and a careful planner. He prefers argument to compromise, and he can be firm and steadfast in his convictions.

Vladimir Putin

President Putin has a mixture of angles and arcades as connecting strokes. He is very much a perfectionist, and with his determination and ambition was destined to become a leader of some sort. However, he is extremely critical by nature. Some of those exaggerated arcades point to a bit of a showman.

You can see above that President Trump and Putin share certain qualities. They probably admire each other's leadership skills as well as tenacity of purpose. They are both stubborn.

Chancellor Merkel is likely to come across as the gentlest of the three and certainly possesses charm and patience, but she is unlikely to prove to be a pushover in negotiations!

Jack Lew

A few years ago I was asked to analyse the signature of the new American Secretary of the US Treasury, Jack Lew, as his quite extraordinary signature was going to be on American bank notes.

This is more of a coiled spring than a signature, and although I will be covering signatures later in the book, I thought it was worth showing you here how someone can actually use just a series of arcade strokes to produce a personal stamp of identity. What do you think this says about him?

Personable but extremely secretive, he is probably discreet and ultra diplomatic. Do you think that the ending stroke after the coiled spring looks as though he may be asking people to keep their distance?

Chapter 11

FORM QUALITY

I was once harangued at a party for having a job that entailed 'judging' people. I am, of course, not judging but analysing personality, but in this modern age of political correctness it is difficult to admit that anything we do or think may involve making judgements about others.

The truth is that, as human beings, we make judgements about others all the time.

We form opinions, whether we like to admit it or not, from how people look, speak, behave and even how they dress. We all choose our 'team' or 'tribe' whether at work, in relationships or even when choosing a seat on the bus.

When analysing handwriting we need to make assessments and judgements about various aspects of the writing that would indicate whether we give a positive or negative slant to what we see.

Form quality is about looking at a handwriting sample holistically without drilling into the detail, and in a similar way making decisions about the overall 'flow' of the script. In time you will also be able to judge form quality just by looking at the script and without examining it closely.

Form quality is assessed on a number of different factors, and a major one being the natural (or forced) rhythm that the writing possesses.

Once again we are looking for balance, with few, if any, exaggerations, elaborate embellishments, a speed that is neither too fast nor too slow, and an individual handwriting that remains legible. This is the ideal and sounds a tall order – right?

Before delving into the nuances of each and every stroke, a high form quality is indicative of above-average intelligence, originality and honesty.

If a form quality is low this does not necessarily mean the writer is of low intelligence, but it could mean that they are more suited to manual labour or to being a team player rather than a leader.

Let's have a look at ways to judge form quality. As I mentioned above, you will see that a big part of it is judging both the writer's common sense when it comes to using space and time, but also using our own visual intuition when interpreting the handwriting.

Height

Look for a good balance between the three zones. Is there tangling of lines? Does one zone hugely dominate the others? Is there anything that looks just out of kilter or exaggerated?

Spacing

How does the writer fill the page? Are the margins fairly even and not top- or bottom-heavy? How is the spacing between the letters, words and lines? Does the writing look well planned, without being too rigidly regular?

Pressure

Is there a natural and healthy pressure to the script? Neither agonisingly heavy nor spidery light?

Remember that writing that is pleasing to the eye is unlikely to be overly embellished but will possess a fluidity and grace without excessive artifice or regularity.

Rhythm and Speed

A high form quality will always possess a level of spontaneity: the writing will not be so slow as to look too precise, and conversely not so fast that it looks neglected and illegible. Have a look at what we have previously discussed, such as broadness of stroke, extended end strokes and other factors that indicate a fast or slow hand.

Regularity

As we are humans and not robots, all of our movements are prone to fluctuation. When judging the regularity of handwriting we are looking to see how many fluctuations exist. Is the size of the letters relatively the same throughout the script? Does the form of connection remain constant? What about the slant, etc.?

In other words, has the writer been able to retain some measure of willpower that results in an individualistic style without an overly rigid and controlled outlook that robs the writer of spontaneity?

We have covered the dynamics of the handwriting that will lead us to make a decision about form quality, but what about the way letters are actually formed – can this help us to judge form quality? The answer is a resounding yes!

As always, be on the lookout for letter formations that immediately appear out of place to the eye due to over-embellishment. Could this be a sign of narcissism? (we will explore this further in Chapter 14) or oversimplification to the point of neglect (could they be avoiding responsibility and even be deceitful?). Let's look in more detail . . .

Enrichment

Why would someone add to or enrich their handwriting with 'extras' such as curlicues or flourishes? It may mean that they have an artistic temperament and like to display their creativity in all areas of their life. Or it could indicate vanity, narcissism and a burning desire to be the centre of attention. A dinner party nightmare, in other words.

Look at me!

Over-embellishment

It is one thing to make a playful gesture, but sometimes an eye-catchingly dramatic, painstakingly embellished writing can be a real red flag for what could be deception and distraction. Think of it as the body language equivalent of the arm-flailing, cape-sweeping con man who is trying to sell you snake oil.

Sadly, I once had a friend who had handwriting like this. I looked forward to his letters because they were a feast for the eyes in terms of flourishes, little pictures, coloured ink and embellishments of all sorts. It must have taken him so long to write one side of paper. He has a lot of time to pursue his letter-writing hobby now as he is in prison for fraud . . .

Simplification with legibility can indicate a high form quality – the writer possesses a speedy mind and originality.

However, when it is so simplified that it becomes unreadable, then the form quality reduces as the writer shows lack of patience, perseverance and a possibly evasive character. This screams 'running away from reality'!

Another thing to look out for is when a handwriting just looks neglected, disorganised and careless. Even if the writer themselves looks neat and tidy, there will be an aspect of their life or their home that is reflected in this handwriting. This won't be a happy, balanced individual.

The opposite of this should also ring an alarm bell.

Always remember – individuality and simplification without ornamentation and neglect is the key to high form quality.

*I do like to be very
neat and upright*

Physical Illness

Both illness and injury to the body can have a huge impact on handwriting and can result in loss of form quality. This may result in rhythmic disturbance, especially when a writer has a condition that causes tremors or muscle degeneration. As I have mentioned in the introduction, don't go there, you are not a doctor.

Transient Anxiety

Remember that our handwriting is prone to minor and subtle changes hour by hour; this is part of the fun of graphology, because as well as analysing character, we can also see how someone is feeling at any given time.

However, trauma and major upset, in a similar way to physical illness, can cause the very fabric of our handwriting to change. If the writer is going through an extremely stressful or worrying episode in their life, the form quality can reflect this.

Exercise 13: Form quality

Can you judge your own form quality? Score yourself highly if you have a good steady rhythm and speed, and simplified but not neglected letter shapes. Remember the spacing and the size – nothing should be too out of kilter.

Which of the samples in each pair below shows a higher overall intelligence and why?

1 A   *Can you see me?*

   B   *Can you see me?*

2 A   *Do you have the time?*

   B   *Do you have the time?*

3 A   *Consistency is key*

   B   *Consistency is key*

4 A   *Let's do it!*

   B   *Let's do it!*

5 A *I loved my school*

B *I loved my school*

6 A *I try to be organised and get things done.*

B *I try to be organised and get things done.*

7 A *Hello there!*

B *Hello there!*

Answers

1) A – Neither neglected nor illegible. The writer can communicate well.

2) B – Fast writing but legible. The writer is able to think speedily.

3) A – The writer shows consistency and rhythm. They are able to adapt to life.

4) B – The size is medium and certainly not over large. They can concentrate easily.

5) B – Not too rigid nor too copybook. The writer shows creativity and independence.

6) B – The spacing and layout is good. This is a sign of great organisational skills.

7) A – Unembellished and free of ornamentation. The writer feels no need to 'cover up' and has spontaneity and a higher IQ.

What does your form quality say about you?

Is your handwriting regular in size, speed and slant?

YES →
YOU SHOW SIGNS OF A WELL-ORGANISED, LOGICAL MIND

Is the regularity very rigid?

YES →
THIS CAN INDICATE A LOWER FORM LEVEL AND A SLOWER, LESS SPONTANEOUS HAND

NO →
Do you have simplified, legible words?

YES →
CONGRATULATIONS, YOU HAVE A HIGH FORM LEVEL WITH HIGH FUNCTIONING INTELLIGENCE

NO →
YOU MAY STILL HAVE A HIGH FORM LEVEL BUT RETAIN A CAUTIOUS, LESS CREATIVE APPROACH TO LIFE

NO →
YOUR FORM LEVEL MAY BE COMPROMISED BY POOR ORGANISATION

Do you have signs of embellishment or ornamentation?

YES →
YOU CAN BE SELF-CONSCIOUS OR EVEN EVASIVE!

NO →
ASSESS INDIVIDUAL CHARACTERISTICS TO GAUGE IF YOU HAVE A LOW FORM QUALITY OR JUST AVERAGE!

WHOSE LINE IS IT ANYWAY?

Charles Dickens

Abraham Lincoln

Pablo Picasso

Charles Dickens

Although Dickens' handwriting shows some irregularity of spacing and size, the script is enriched while retaining legibility. The writer is hugely creative, but a complex character. The form level manages to remain high.

Abraham Lincoln

Lincoln shows a high form level with speedy, original writing. Despite the more formal writing of the time, he still shows short forms without compromising legibility.

Pablo Picasso

This is a tricky one as the handwriting could seem neglected, with irregular size, baseline and spacing, as well as extreme simplification of letters making legibility challenging (to say the least).

Picasso's creative genius and emotional volatility are both evident, as is his refusal to conform to other people's idea of normality, and that includes graphological form quality.

Here are examples of three mass murderers. All three of them have low form quality – can you identify why?

that won hardly (laughly).....sh (:) ... bitches! So-to-speak. And ... I know it was only a fantasy joyable to debate the pros and cons of with other guys who'd had their own fantasies)) Yeah ... raw vInIsm to the max! (but I want to prison for a rape I didn't commit! Yeah!, I'm still as that — but I didn't go looking for her (a stunning blonde, by-the-way!) when I got out!!.) OH!,. wisdom of hindsight afterhand !!!

Roy Norris

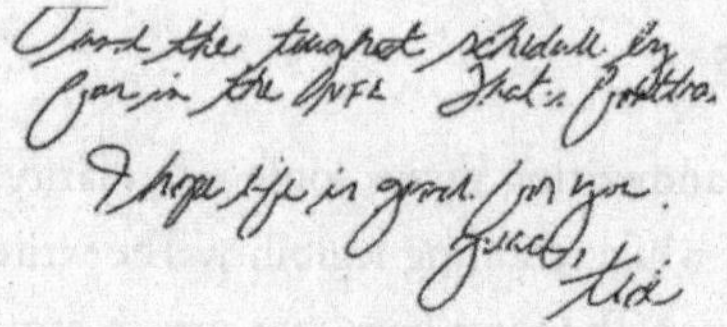

[handwritten note]

Ted Bundy

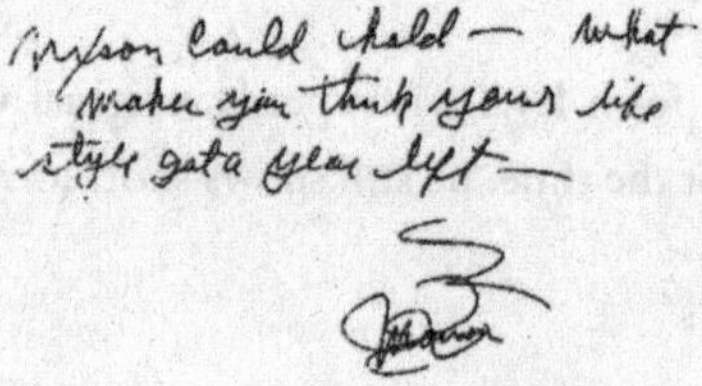

[handwritten note]

Charles Manson

Roy Norris

Norris displays a writing that is full of underlinings, exclamation marks and other unnecessary additions. He also rigidly sticks to an overly regular slant, letter formation and spacing. The ultra-straight baseline helps us to assess his calculated manipulation alongside his childish need for attention. There is also evidence of extremely heavy and pasty writing, which can indicate violence in some cases.

Ted Bundy

Bundy shows a rigid, extreme right slant coupled with neglected, tangled writing and overly long lower loops. The form quality is low, showing a personality that is confused and self-obsessed, and has an uncontrollable physical appetite with violent tendencies.

Charles Manson

Extreme irregularity as well as neglect point to a low form quality and an emotionally volatile individual. The signature, which is partially crossed out by his own affected ornamentation, shows both narcissism but also a masked low self-esteem.

Hopefully you won't come across many handwritings like these in your life . . .

Chapter 12

LEAD-IN AND END STROKES

We have looked at the correlation between body language and graphology and, in much the same way that we all consciously or subconsciously make our own entrance into or indeed exit out of a room, we can see how a person might want to make some kind of similar statement when writing. They may want to make a pen stroke of some kind at the beginning and ending of each word.

In the UK the writing style that we are taught at school has few lead-in strokes while European and American handwriting styles tend to have longer lead-ins. Do you think this may be indicative of cultural and social differences between nations? Rethink this question when you have come to the end of this chapter!

Brits just love to get on with it.

you crazy British - slow down

Do you need a lot of time to prepare before every action, or do you just leap into situations?

Whether you creep in or parachute naked down the chimney, let's have a look at the different types of lead-in strokes to begin with.

No Lead-in

just crack on with it!

As you can probably imagine, these writers have speedy thought processes and don't need lengthy preparation or others' approval. They are nearly always independent and self-assured. This trait could be an indication of high form level.

Garland Lead-in

please like me

Remember the garland shape? These writers will take their time to be warm and welcoming towards others, while still retaining normal social boundaries.

Overly Long Garland Lead-in

I'm absolutely hilarious

These people are like the garland lead-in ones, but with an element of exhibitionism. In their eagerness to be liked, they can be distractingly amusing or deeply irritating, depending on your state of mind.

Garland Lead-in From The Upper Zone

hugely Intelligent

This writer takes the time to make sure others know exactly how mentally superior he or she is. Look for other factors such as the overly tall upper zone or perhaps other embellishments that point to a smoke screen.

Arcade Lead-in

black sheep of the family

They may not actually be the black sheep of the family, but arcade lead-in writers often see themselves as a bit different and tend to be secretive about their personal life. They are unlikely to be overly influenced by others.

Arcade Lead-in Towards The Upper Zone

I'm a Unicorn

Here we have someone with great imagination, or a fantasist. Take your pick.

Angle Lead-in

I haven't chosen my family

There is an edge to these people: they can have excellent memories but can also find it difficult to let go of a grudge, or indeed they can take delight in seeking one out.

Angle Lead-in Towards The Upper Zone

Who and Why and What?

This betrays an analytical and probing mind. Such a writer tends to be the questioner of the universe and would make a great private investigator.

Thread Lead-in

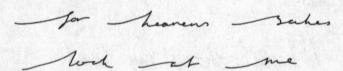

These people are hesitant and indecisive; you just don't know if they're coming in or staying out.

Overly Long Thread Lead-in

Like all writers who have long lead-in strokes, these individuals need attention and may well enjoy a little drama. Look at them dragging their cloak behind them so that the door has to be kept open for their grand entrance!

Hook Lead-in

If the lead-in strokes look like small hooks as opposed to fully formed garland strokes, then this points to a clannish individual who may find it hard to give up on things or people. They don't like change.

Tick Lead-in

just eff off and let me work!

Wherever you see small tick-like strokes (as opposed to the larger angled lead-in), then you can be sure that the writer feels irritable and sharp-tempered. This may be temporary but it's probably best to leave them alone for a while to cool down.

Hesitant and Repetitive Lead-in

um... um... oh never mind.

These writers are so hesitant and unsure of themselves that you will probably see their pen or pencil hover a little while before they actually get cracking with what they want to write. There might even be a few false starts. Apart from making a mess on the paper, these people can often fail to achieve what they deserve in life through uncertainty and unnecessary caution.

Now have a look at your own handwriting. What do you see? Do you have a no-nonsense, no-lead-in sort of writing or the dramatic entrance of an actor? Or are you trying to put off what you really need to say?

Try writing with the reverse of what you are used to. If you have no lead-in strokes normally, then grab a pen and draw them. Have a look at the shape – are they garland, arcade, angle or thread? What does this say about you?

Do the reverse if you normally have lead-in strokes. Just put the pen to the paper with no mucking around and get writing. Do you feel bereft? Rushed? Unprepared?

Exercise 14 : Lead-in Strokes

Which of these two would you ring in an emergency?

A   *I'm coming to help you.*

B   *I'm coming in my own time.*

Not much of a test – the answer is A. By the time B has got to your house, the fire will have engulfed you. And then they realise they've left their cape behind . . .

Who's more likely to be telling the truth?

A   *I'm An Astronaut*

B   *I'm an astronaut*

They may well both be lying, but B is the more cautious of the two and less prone to fantasy. Leave A behind on terra firma.

What do your lead-in strokes say about you?

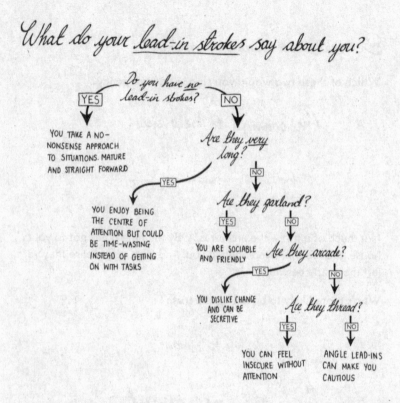

Now let's have a look at end strokes.

As we finish one word and before we start another, it may seem quite natural to end the word with more than a blunt ending.

Do you have a natural garlanded ending which looks as though you are embracing the next word, or do you have a less-than-friendly long thread stroke which visually looks as though you are keeping others at arm's length?

No End Strokes

You look dreadful

These people can be relied upon to have an independent mind and good powers of concentration. They don't need others' approval, which is just as well because they can be a bit blunt.

Short Club-like End Strokes

you look shocking

These people can be cruel and hurtful. Red flag!

Garland End Strokes

you look fine

Here you have someone who is friendly and open.

Overly Long Garland End Strokes

you look truly great

This person is perhaps a bit too friendly. Ask yourself, what are they after?

Thread End Strokes

yeh_____ yeh_____ whatever_____

Those long strokes look as though they are pushing something away, and it could be other people . . . or even you.

Upward End Strokes

you look like a unicorn

A dreamer, a philosopher, or just a fantasist?

Leftward End Strokes

stop looking at me

If the end strokes resemble an umbrella or a cover for the preceding letters then you can be assured that the writer feels self-protective or at a disadvantage in some way.

End Strokes That Cross Through a Word

I'm looking bad

This is quite often seen in a signature, which we will cover with greater detail in Chapter 16, but if many words look as though they have been crossed out with the end stroke, this has a negative connotation. The writer feels bad about themselves.

Angled End Strokes

you look O.K I guess

Angled end strokes, whether they are protracted or just look like ticks, are a sign of a temper and a critical attitude, so only ask these writers' opinion when you really want to know it.

Arcade End Strokes

I can't tell you how you look

These people are just a little secretive.

Downward End Strokes

I just don't care how you look

This indicates intolerance and a tendency to think in rather black and white terms . . . Ouch.

Embellished Endings

you look fabulous darling

Like all forms of over-embellishment (see Chapter 11, 'Form Quality'), these people are best taken with a large pinch of salt.

As you can see, there is a very wide variety of different end strokes and, with a bit of practice and a lot of examining of handwriting, you will soon spot the different forms of both lead-in and end strokes and make your own judgement.

Now have a good look at your own end strokes. Do you have any and, if so, do they fit into a category above?

Try playing around with a variety of different end strokes, from short and blunt to long and sweeping. Do you feel differently when you change your endings?

Exercise 15: **End Strokes**

Which of these two would you be most wary of?

A *Hom are you?*

B *How are you?*

You should be most keen to keep A at a distance. Those blunt endings could spell danger.

Who would you employ to work on the reception desk?

A *Do come in*

B *Do come in*

Writer A is the correct answer because B appears far from welcoming.

How would you give this person some honest advice?

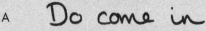
What have I done wrong?

The answer is very carefully and diplomatically, because they have leftward end strokes which means that they are defensive and are likely to assume they are in the wrong from the get-go.

What do your <u>end strokes</u> say about you?

Do you have <u>no</u> end strokes?

YES

YOU HAVE GOOD MENTAL CONCENTRATION AND ARE INDEPENDENT

NO

Are they <u>very</u> long?

YES

YOU CAN BE FRIENDLY AND OPEN BUT TOO LONG AND THE REVERSE IS TRUE

NO

Do they rise up?

YES

YOU MAY BE A BIT OF A DREAMER OR IDEALIST

NO

Do they reach down to lower zone?

YES

WATCH FOR INTOLERANCE

NO

IF THEY ARE OF AVERAGE LENGTH AND PROPORTION THEN YOU HAVE NORMAL, HEALTHY DRIVES.

WHOSE LINE IS IT ANYWAY?

You phenominal Ladies

Love Beyoncé

Beyoncé

To Film —
Happy Birthday
"#50"
Joe Travolta

John Travolta

note, it made my
day - Best wish,

Warren Buffett

Vincent van Gogh

Beyoncé

This super-famous singer takes a direct approach to life, with short end strokes and virtually no lead-in strokes. She knows her own mind, is independent and tells it how it is!

John Travolta

John Travolta displays angled lead-in strokes to the upper zone and an arcaded end stroke.

He has an inquisitive and probing mind but is more secretive and guarded about his own life.

Warren Buffett

Look at those sweeping, arcaded lead-in strokes and the arcaded end strokes.

Mr Buffett is extremely guarded and self-possessed. He certainly knows his own mind, but is a traditionalist at heart.

Vincent van Gogh

Notwithstanding that this is an archaic style of writing, van Gogh shows us a variety of garland end strokes as well as a self-protective end stroke to his letter 'd'. He is responsive and warm, but also feels a need to protect his own interests. Do you think he felt that he had the recognition that he deserved in his lifetime?

Chapter 13

CONNECTION AND DISCONNECTION

This chapter does not refer to an unpaid utility bill, but rather the degree to which we connect our letters within a word.

In the West we are taught to connect our letters when we write. Most of us go on to disconnect some of our letters, whether we are merely pausing to gather our thoughts or through unconscious habit, but some people write in a completely disconnected way.

Along with most things in life, writing is a process of stopping and starting, breathing in, breathing out, putting the brake on and taking the brake off.

I was once told that there is a correlation between the degree to which people connect their letters and the fluidity of their speech. We all know hesitant talkers, those that pause often during a sentence. These people like to take their time over what they have to say. Fast-talkers, gabblers, those that don't pause for breath, could find the slow speakers very tiresome and frustrating to listen to.

But what does it all mean? The degree of connection between letters allows us to gauge the writer's thought processes and mental abilities. If you refer back to Chapter 9, 'Speed', you will be reminded that it is speedier to write with connected letters. Every time we take the pen off the paper – even for a millisecond – our writing slows down.

As we have seen, it is quite 'normal' to take our pen off the paper in order to cross our 't's or dot 'i's but some people don't even do that. Indeed, some speedy connective writers even connect their words! More on that later. In the meantime let's examine what it means to write with what we will refer to as 'average' connected writing.

Connected Writing

When most of the letters in the word are linked with just breaks for 't' bars and 'i' dots, then the writing is considered to be 'connected'.

one step at a time is best

These writers tend to use logic and reason over intuition. In the same way that their pens move relatively seamlessly over the paper, their mind is able to plan and sequence their daily activities. They enjoy order and generally have good powers of concentration.

In a work situation, they can be relied upon to have a clear-cut idea of how to bring a project to fruition and to work through it with clarity. In short, they are the well-organised diary keepers who can be relied upon to deliver to a deadline.

The downside of this is that they tend to analyse everything, including their own feelings, which can be tiresome for the more creative types.

They need constant mental stimulation to keep them happy as they will get bored and restless easily if they have nothing to do.

They are definitely the people to go to if you need practical advice, but more sensitive types may find them a little too matter-of-fact and blunt.

OVER-CONNECTION

cant stop now its a routine

When the handwriting is overly connected, to the extent that the pen isn't even lifted off the paper to pause to cross 't's or dot 'i's, then you can be sure that concentration on the matter in hand is so great that the writer is unable to switch tack or contemplate distraction.

Communicative? Yes, but severe antipathy to change can really limit this person.

CONNECTION BETWEEN WORDS

Im never giving up on you

Sometimes you will come across a writer who not only joins up the letters, but also actually joins up the words on the page, a bit like a line of washing.

Powers of concentration are second to none here, as is the ability to follow a strategy to get what this person wants. There is nearly always an eccentricity to this personality and they can be creative in their own peculiar way.

Look to see what you think of his or her form level and gauge whether they have the ability to concentrate on what's important. Do they possess a less than positive quality of obsessional tendencies? I don't know why, but Kathy Bates in *Misery* springs to mind

PARTIAL CONNECTION

Frankly I can take you or leave you.

This is very common, and most of us have partial connectedness between letters. The pen is taken off the paper in order to cross 't's and dot 'i's and sometimes in other places. However, the natural flow of the writing is not interrupted.

Spontaneous but creative as well, these writers are able to be both logical and intuitive.

FALSE CONNECTION

more creative than I let on

At first glance, this writing looks connected but in fact the writer has lifted the pen or pencil off the paper but replaced it to follow the line.

To all intents and purposes this is connected writing, although the writer is hiding their intuitive and creative side under a bushel of conformity.

Disconnected Writing

disconnect

As we've discussed, most of us write with a mix of connected and disconnected letters because this is what feels natural to most people. However, some of us write with mainly disconnected or totally disconnected writing, much like a printed document.

The flow of writing is constantly interrupted and the script may appear somewhat jerky and unnecessarily punctuated. In some cases, letters really seem isolated from one another.

Disconnected writers tend to be intuitive. As long as the letters aren't actually isolated from each other and if the writing still looks fluid in its own way, then these writers can be highly creative.

They are able to reflect on what they have seen or experienced, and come up with novel approaches to problems. Once again, have a look at the form quality of the writing itself: the higher the overall form quality, then the more positive the interpretation.

We can subdivide disconnection as follows:

DISCONNECTED BUT NOT 'PRINTED' WRITING

I just know I hate you . . .

We are looking for instances here where most of the letters are detached from each other, with some cursive or taught letter formations.

These people certainly act from feeling rather than intellect, and they often claim to just 'know' things. Grabbing ideas and concepts from nowhere, they are nevertheless observant and intuitive.

They are likely to have a good imagination but, negatively, can form strong opinions with little logic to back them up. These emotional types are not everybody's cup of tea and can easily rub others up the wrong way, but on the other hand their conclusions can often be spot on. They are investigative types, but not the most socially diplomatic.

DISCONNECTED AND HIGHLY ORIGINAL WRITING

and (really don't care .

These people are like the disconnected but not 'printed' writers, but with an added zest of highly creative and even genius-like individuality. They judge others speedily and form opinions rapidly. They are unlikely to get too hung up about what others think of them.

PRINTED WRITING

I'm better off working on my own

The writing is carefully and slowly formed with definite spaces between each letter. The writer does not always feel self-confident and, for a variety of reasons, has a need to print out what he or she is trying to say.

In graphology, this has all the signs of a 'mask' or cover-up for feelings of insecurity. They have a tendency to not conform, isolate themselves from others for fear of being judged, and can then become lonely and critical of themselves and others.

Conversely, they can be perfectionists in whatever they do.

Individualistic or hermit-like . . . What else does their writing say about them to help you decide?

PRINTING WITH CAPITAL LETTERS

I'D LIKE TO TELL YOU TO...

Here the writer is making it very clear that they want to be understood. The trouble is that sometimes the message is that they can be self-absorbed and even insensitive to the feelings of others.

However, there are different reasons why people decide to print – even in capital letters. Sometimes it is for practical reasons, such as . . .

The writer feels that their natural writing is illegible . . .

If you happen to have handwriting that is poorly formed and largely illegible, then you may print for the sake of legibility. Read the message carefully. If the writer is writing something important, such as instructions which need to be followed to the letter (pun intended), then he or she may very well print so that there is no misunderstanding.

Or . . .

The writer is hiding their personality . . .

If you or someone you know is perfectly capable of and known to write with a normal cursive script, then it may be that they are covering up a facet or facets of their personality.

It is much quicker to write with joined-up writing, so why would someone actually choose to use a disconnected script? A bit like a mask at a ball or fancy dress party, the writer has consciously or unconsciously chosen to hide the real them. Or . . .

The writer occupationally prints . . .

What exactly am I talking about?! Some occupations such as engineers, architects and surveyors demand a printed form of writing on blueprints and plans. After a while this type of writing becomes the 'norm' for this person.

LOOK AT MY building

Do look out for other telltale signs of a person who has a talent for design or architecture.

SPECIFIC WORDS ARE PRINTED

I really LOVE you

Just LISTEN to what I say

As with all handwriting anomalies, look at which words are highlighted. Do the words that are printed have a resonance with the writer, even if he or she doesn't actually know it?

It's a bit like shouting.

DISCONNECTION OF STROKES WITHIN LETTERS THEMSELVES

YOU'LL NEVER KNOW ME!

Visually odd and disjointed, this extremely slow writing takes a sinister twist.

The writer has gone to the ponderous lengths of disconnecting every stroke of the letters. This is more than a cover-up, and a red flag for possible criminal tendencies.

Thinking before acting is one thing, but this is indicative of a devious and calculating mind.

Exercise 16: Connecting and Disconnecting

Which of these two is the faster writer?

A *Speedy Gonzales*   B *Speedy Gonzales*

The answer is A. Disconnection always slows the writer down. The faster writer in this case is more logical than intuitive.

Who is telling the truth?

A I'm a logical type

B I'm a logical type

It's B. If you remember, the joined-up letters signify logical, orderly thinking as opposed to the writer who grabs ideas from nowhere, or blue-sky thinkers as we refer to them now.

Which of these three finds it easiest to make friends?

A I LOVE a party

B I love a party

C I love a party

This is, of course, a hard one to be sure about because it depends on what the party is like and who is attending! However, out of the three of them, C has the most obviously balanced personality and is naturally outgoing.

Writer A is more of the eccentric loner and B may find it harder to integrate because their intensity and their originality may not be appreciated by everyone.

Who are you more likely to trust as a babysitter?

A   I'M A BABYSITTER

B   *I'm a babysitter*

Both of these writers have disconnected writing, but whereas B is a creative, intuitive type, A is a little too sinister to be trusted unless they are auditioning for a part in *The Hand that Rocks the Cradle*. In which case – they've got the job.

What about your own writing? Are you a connected logical type or a disconnected blue-sky thinker? Try pushing yourself and writing in a different connective style. Does it slow you down or speed you up?

What does your <u>connection/disconnection</u> say about you?

Is your handwriting mainly connected?

YES

YOU ARE LOGICAL, RATIONAL AND COMMUNICATIVE

Is it totally connected?

YES

YOU HAVE GREAT POWERS OF CONCENTRATION BUT MAY NOT BE USED TO USING INTUITION

NO

YOU ARE WELL BALANCED AND THOUGHTFUL BUT NOT OVERLY PONDEROUS

NO

Is it printed and totally disconnected?

YES

IT IS IMPORTANT THAT YOU ARE UNDERSTOOD BY OTHERS

NO

YOU ARE HIGHLY INTUITIVE WITH ORIGINAL THOUGHTS AND IDEAS

WHOSE LINE IS IT ANYWAY?

*your wife which I haven't had
the chance to do
Sincerely,
Bob De Niro*

Robert De Niro

*Here's to you and
your family!*

Sir Richard Branson

*Hi Debbie Tranx
4 coming on the show 2
talk about your boyfriends
small penis problem*

Ellen DeGeneres

*Hopefully we can work together
again. love Leo*

Leonardo DiCaprio

Robert De Niro

This award-winning actor and director displays a carefully formed and well-balanced hand with a connected letter form style.

He is highly communicative and friendly, but thoughtful with a logical view of life. Can you also spot the form of connection? That combination of thread and angle suggests originality and intelligence.

Sir Richard Branson

Sir Richard Branson also shows a connected style, but with a vertical slant and a tall upper zone.

Sir Richard is a great strategist and planner but also possesses a strong imagination. He is extremely focused and ambitious, and has the foresight and ability to carry his ideas to fruition.

Ellen DeGeneres

Ellen has chosen to write in a disconnected hand but without capital letters.

Ellen has small spaces between both the letters and words, as well as disconnecting the actual letters. She is creative, humorous and intuitive, but she is also less outgoing than people may think, and may even be a little bit shy off-camera.

Leonardo DiCaprio

Another disconnector, but this writing is less regular. Leonardo is highly creative and artistic, but has the artist's more volatile personality. The letters are spaced far apart, and the letters themselves are fairly wide. He can be outgoing and expansive, and enjoys the spotlight. The perfect attributes for an actor!

What else can you deduce from his handwriting? How do you think he was feeling when writing this?

Chapter 14

THE PERSONAL PRONOUN

ME, ME, ME . . .

'I' and the way we write it is certainly significant enough to warrant the personal pronoun its own chapter. When we write 'I' we are not just writing any old letter of the alphabet but we are, in effect, displaying ourselves, our ego, our self-image and how we place ourselves in the world around us.

Unlike other languages, English just uses the one letter to represent the personal pronoun, and when writing it, it can stand visually in splendid isolation, with nothing to support it or hide behind: it can really stand out on the page, particularly if written after a major event in the writer's life, whether joyous or traumatic. Or it could meld perfectly with the rest of the script.

When looking at your own written personal pronoun or that of others, treat it as an entire word. There can be so much to unpack. As we grow older and mature we still express our needs and wants, but they can become more hidden and harder to unravel. However, by looking at the way an 'I' is written, you will have a heads-up as to how someone sees themselves and what they really want in life. Consider every facet that we have learned so far.

The spacing: how is it placed in relation to other words? The size: is it obviously bigger or smaller than other words on the page? The pressure: is it heavier or lighter than the rest of the script? Finally and very importantly, how is the 'I' actually written: is it straight up and down, curled in on itself or does it possess a sharp, angry angle?

Remember, as with all handwriting, a personal pronoun on a page is liable to fickle changes of slant, pressure or size depending on how the writer is feeling about himself or herself at the time. As always, be observant also for changes within just one sample of writing . . .

Without further ado, let's have a closer look at the different 'I's that you may come across and what they reveal.

The Stick Figure

I am frightfully independent.

The writer of this 'I' has given a single straight line to represent themselves; there is no embellishment or need for them to justify their existence. This person is independent in nature, mature and without artifice.

The Column

I am frightfully cultured

Topped and tailed and still linear, this personal pronoun stands out but still looks refined. Here we have someone who is cultured, constructive in their thinking and who has a desire to be noticed without being narcissistic.

The Lower Case

i am frightfully passive aggressive

This is perhaps a little unfair, but it feels like the sheer understatement and 'I'm not important enough for a capital letter' vibe here may indicate quite the reverse.

The Upper Loop

I am frightfully important

In Chapter 3 we discussed loops in the upper zone, and here the writer has a strong need to put his feelings on display. This person feels superior: they're a showman or show-woman. They have a strong imagination, particularly when it comes to their own importance!

The Lower Loop

I am frightfully sexy

Once again, refer back to Chapter 3, 'The Zones', and you will see that this writer is so strongly sensually driven that their sexual and physical desire and imagination has also become part of their outward persona.

The Sword

I am frightfully aggressive

This person always knows best, is irritable, critical or even aggressive. You can see this from the sword-like, cutting effect.

The Open Cradle

I am frightfully vulnerable.

Unlike the 'sword', the 'open cradle' has curled in on itself for safety. This writer feels insecure and self-protective, but they can also be chatty.

The Encircled

O am frightfully risk averse

Similar to the 'open cradle', but even more self-protective and even a little paranoid. Extremely cautious, this person is unlikely to be a lion-tamer.

The Curlicue

E am frightfully vulgar

This personal pronoun looks vulgar and very unnatural. I'd say we have someone here who is pretentious, eccentric and probably lacking in aesthetic sensibilities.

The Needle

I am frightfully controlling

As the shape and name suggest, this writer has chosen a narrow and straight loop, similar to the 'Upper Loop' but less full of bravado and exaggeration. He or she needs to be in charge. They are more idealistic than realistic.

The Swinger

I am frightfully emotional

Similar to the writers of open lower-zone loops, these people are emotional, sentimental and friendly. They may or may not actually be swingers.

The Tick

I am frightfully irritable

All unnecessary ticks on letters are a sign of mostly transitory irritation. This writer has made it part of their USP. Beware of the short fuse! This person is charming, but is not to be goaded.

The Retraced

I am frightfully repressed

Retracing points to someone who is anxious, repressed and lacking in confidence. They have had to go over what they have already written, 'just to be sure'.

The Money Bags

$ am frightfully rich and so am £

The very obvious imagery speaks for itself. We're dealing with someone who is single-minded here!

Size Differences

I am thinking about myself and i wish i was more important

No prizes for guessing who has the overinflated ego and who suffers from an inferiority complex. Remember that the size is judged in relation to the rest of the script.

Spacing Differences

I choose to live alone and like it that way but I also crave company.

When the personal pronoun stands isolated and far from the preceding and following word, then the writer has chosen to stand apart from others or may have just become used to their isolation.

If the personal pronoun is crammed up against other words, it's fair to say that the writer has a fear of being alone.

Pressure Differences

I feel under pressure even when I feel tired.

Look at the pressure of the writing as a whole. Does the personal pronoun differ from the rest? If it shows heavier pressure than the main body of text, then it is likely that the writer feels the pressure of life on their shoulders. If it is obviously lighter than the rest of the text, then this indicates that the writer feels inwardly unsure of themselves.

Slant Differences

When the slant of the personal pronoun matches that of the rest of the text, such writers feel no conflict between how they feel and how they behave.

I am what I am

A right-slanted personal pronoun with a left-slanted script indicates an inwardly confident and friendly writer who cannot for whatever reason express this in public. Look at the contents of the letter or who they were writing to for clues.

I am trying to appear hesitant

A leftward-sloping personal pronoun in a right-slanted script indicates another conflict: a cautious, inward-looking individual who is putting on a more outgoing front to the world. See if you can detect why this would be.

I really do feel confident!

What does your 'I' say about you? Look back at old samples of your writing – has the way you've written it changed?

Compare your personal pronoun to those of the people you live or work with. Do you think your self-images are a match or a clash?

Exercise 17: The Personal Pronoun

What do you think the writer really feels about this person?

I   am so looking forward
to seeing you tomorrow.

Answer: The writer is naturally a bit of a loner (look at the spacing) and is feeling irritable (look at the tick), so I'm not totally convinced of the truth behind their message.

Which of these writers is best suited to a career in architecture?

A   *I love buildings*

B   *I love buildings*

C   *I love buildings*

Answer: The answer is B. That column suggests a love of form and construction.

How close is this couple?

My wife   and I

Answer: Not very, I think! 'Wife' is written with a leftward slant and is literally kept at a distance from the personal pronoun and the writer. However, there is a very small space between 'and' and 'I', which suggests that the writer also craves closeness. Not from their wife, presumably . . .

Truth or Lie?

I have little interest in money

Answer: Seriously?

WHOSE LINE IS IT ANYWAY?

What can you deduce about these personalities from their personal pronouns?

I never think about my style

Lucian Freud

*MAY I ~~SAY~~ HAPPY 70th ANNIVERSARY.
THAT IS AN EXTRAORDINARY MILESTONE FOR
WHICH YOU SHOULD*

George Clooney

I am writing you a letter

Mick Jagger

Lucian Freud

Lucian Freud's 'I' is a straightforward, no-nonsense stick figure but it also has a slight left slant to it compared to the main text. There are also signs that the pressure is lighter than the main body of writing.

Freud was certainly an independent and, some would say, eccentric thinker and artist, but the slight left slant and lighter pressure indicate that he was not a raging egomaniac and had a more straightforward view of himself, as well as being highly sensitive.

George Clooney

This Hollywood heart-throb uses a column personal pronoun. Apart from his obvious physical charms, he is straight-talking, mature and is likely to have a visual flair for symmetry.

What do you think the way that he has printed his letters says about him, and does it contradict or complement my analysis?

Mick Jagger

This musical genius possesses a retraced and large upper loop on his personal pronoun. He is a little vain perhaps, but also the retracing suggests caution and repression.

See if you can find other samples of Mick Jagger's writing. Does his personal pronoun change over the years?

Chapter 15

LETTER SPECIFICS
(THE A–Z OF GRAPHOLOGY)

As we know, when analysing handwriting it is important to understand that although all facets of the writing are important, a picture of the personality can only be drawn together when the handwriting is looked at as a whole.

Having said that, we can also study all the individual letters of the alphabet and the different ways in which they can be written, to understand what is truly unique about someone's personality.

It would be impossible for me to go through the alphabet and show every single variation of how a letter can be written. If I did then this one book would turn into dozens of directories!

Instead, I'm going to show you a few of the more common ways of writing each letter of the alphabet and what this can reveal about the writer.

Remember to bring together everything you have learned so far to understand the shape, size and spacing of letters.

Here goes . . .

A a

A	Simplified	Mature and well-balanced
A	High and narrow	Vain
A	Knotted stroke	Cautious
a	Closed	Modest, unassuming
a	Open	Talkative
a	Knotted	Secretive
a	Knotted and open	Can be creative with the truth

B b

B	Simple copybook	Perfectionist
B	Disconnected strokes	Artistic, visually minded
B	Extended strokes	Determined

ℬ	Embellished	Fantasist
↳	Copybook	In adults, a conformist
♭	Tick	Impatient
₿	Large loop	Arrogant
₿	Ink-filled loop	Sensual

C c

C	Large, rounded	Kind
C	Curled	Self-protective
Ɛ	Knotted	Calculating
(	Narrow, thin	Mean
⌣	Resting on its base	Lazy
C	Nearly closed	Very shy, defensive

D d

	Closed	Discreet
	Open at the top	Chatty
	Looped	Reserved
	Separate strokes	Eccentric
	Angular	Bad-tempered
	Curved formation	Egotistical
	Greek formation	Literary, imaginative
	Open at the base	Careless
	Open at the top	Quick-thinking
	Very large loop	Overly emotional
	Tepee formation	Stubborn

E e

ε	Greek capital	Cultured
ε	Embellished	Vulgar
E	Narrow, thin	Shy
E	Longer middle stroke	Reserved
E	Longer lower stroke	Determined
ϵ	Alternative Greek formation	Cultured
e	Well balanced	Honest
e	Ink-filled	Sensual
l	Narrow	Secretive
e	Rising end stroke	Quick-thinking
e	Angular	Calculating

F f

	Long top bar	Protective
	Angular	Harsh
	Long second stroke	Caution
	Disconnected strokes	Unrealistic
	Archaic and reversed	Stuck in the past
	Wide upper loop	Emotional
	Wide lower loop	Sensual, physical
	Simplified	Intelligent, quick-witted
	Knotted	Secretive
	Ink-filled	Sensual
	Sword-like	Harbouring repressed violence!
	Triangle formation	Hidden anger

G g

	Single downstroke	Quick-thinking
	Table formation	Practical
	Tick on capital	Physically frustrated
	Hook to left	Greedy
	Short downstroke	Critical, analytical
	Overly long downstroke	Sensual
	Short downstroke	Lacking in physical energy
	Loop through middle zone	Overindulgent
	Hook	Family-orientated
	Complicated loops	Sexually vain
	Tick to right	Altruistic
	Triangle	Nag!
	End stroke to right	Physically frustrated

$\mathcal{G}$	Cradling	Maternal
$g \, g \, g$	Variety of downstrokes	Lack of physical control
q	Like figure 9	Materialistic
8	Like figure 8	Literary

H h

H	Narrow	Shy
H	Wide	Extravagant
$\mathcal{H}$	Embellished	Vain and vulgar
H	Angular	Aggressive
T	Long lower strokes	Stubborn
H	Looped	Obsessive
h	Simplified	Refined
$\mathcal{h}$	Tall, rounded loop	Imaginative

♄	Short loop	Humble
♄	Angular	Obstinate
h	Short upper stroke	Lack of intellectual interest
♭	Tall upper stroke	Idealistic
♫	Long lead-in stroke	Critical, cautious

I i

|	Simplistic	Clear-minded
I	Columned	Independent
╎	Pointed	Emotional
⌡	Tick	Concise
⌐	Arcaded	Self-protective
∪	No dot	Careless
∪	Dot to left	Procrastinator

⸜	Dot to right	Impatient
⸜	Circular dot	Immature (in adults)
⸜	Dot-like dash	Bad-tempered

J j

⌡	Large loop	Physically restless
�⅃	Long horizontal stroke	Self-protective
⅁	Like figure 4	Critical of others
⌐⌡	Detached horizontal stroke	Self-deceit
†	Like crucifix	Religious interests
⅁	Large upper-zone loop	Fantasist
✝	Angular	Has a short fuse
⌡	Hooked	Greedy
j	High dot	Very imaginative

K k

⋉	Knotted	Perfectionist and secretive
K	Disconnected	Has poor organisational skills
ℝ	Large loop	Theatrical
⋋	Lower-zone extension	Stubborn, defiant
k	Tall stem	Intellectual vanity
k—	Horizontal extension	Arrogant
k	Narrow or retraced loop	Inhibited
faKe	Large 'K' in middle of word	Attention-seeking
lc	Two separate strokes	Quick-witted

L l

L	Simplified	Refined
ℒ	Looped like £ or $ sign	Money-minded
ℓ	Embellished	Greedy, vain
I	Stick-figure capital	Confident, egotistical
l	Tall loop	Proud
l	Broad loop	Imaginative
∪	Short upper zone	Has little interest in intellectual concerns
l	Ink-filled	Sensual
l	Tick or angle at base	Easily irritated

M m

	Second 'hump' larger or higher	Attention-seeking
	First 'hump' larger or higher	Egotistical
	Square formation	Constructive
	High lead-in stroke	Idealistic
	Long finishing stroke	Very stubborn
	Arcaded	Tactful
	Angled	Insightful, analytical
	Garlanded	Friendly, warm
	Looped	Secretive
	Thread-like	Flaky, indecisive

N n

⑊	Disconnected	Emotionally out of kilter
N	Long final stroke	Enthusiastic, brave
⑂	Long downstroke	Stubborn
ℕ	Embellished	Creative, artistic
♫	Like musical note	Musical!
η	Narrow	Shy
∩	Broad	Extravagant
n	Not reaching baseline	Fearful
↙	Retraced and pointy	Friendly but non-committal
ℳ	Tick end stroke	Irritable

O o

○	Large but neatly formed	Discreet, mature
◡	Open at the top	Indiscreet, chatty
◠	Open at the base	Hypocritical
⦾	Looped	Secretive
⦿	Double looped	Evasive
◖	Encircled	Defensive
0	Narrow	Reserved, has a small ego
⟋σ	Long lead-in stroke	Uber-cautious
( )	Two separate strokes	Nonconformist
⟠	Like an eye	Passive-aggressive

P p

	Large loop	Highly egotistical
	Very tall	Proud
	Square	Interested in all things mechanical
	Angled	Humourless
	Looped stem	Sensual
	Two separate strokes	Visual
	Pointed stem	Ambitious
	Long lower zone, no loop	Energetic
	Long lower zone with loop	Highly sexual
	Open oval	Conformist
	Angled lead-in	Argumentative

Q q

Q	Heavy stem	Aggressive
Q	Open at top	Chatty
Q	Open at base	Dishonest
Q	Looped	Vain
q	Enrolled	Very secretive
q	Short lower zone	Physically weak
q	Long end stroke	Vain
q	Reversed stroke	Non-conformist
q	Long clubbed stroke, no tick	Sexually frustrated

R r

R	Simplified	Well-balanced
R	Inflated loop	Outgoing but needs admiration
R	Long end stroke	Stubborn, obstinate
R	Looped	Secretive
Ro	Contrived	Vain
V	Reaching upwards	Intelligent, content
r	Simplified	Mature
⌐	Flat top	Interested in all things mechanical
⌡	Looped stem	Reserved
2	Like figure 2	Mathematical
—	Thread	Evasive
ŋ	Very curly	Daydreamer

S s

$\int$	Simplified	Independent
$\mathcal{S}$	Embellished	Vulgar (or a fourteenth-century monk!)
$\mathcal{Y}$	Archaic	Old-fashioned
$	Like $ sign	What do you think?!
$\lessgtr$	Angular	Aggressive
$\mathcal{S}$	Long end stroke	Prevaricator
$\oint$	Like musical note	Guess!
$\mathcal{I}$	Sharp top	Critical, sharp-tongued
$\mathcal{L}$	Long end stroke	Keeps others away

T t

$\top$	High, detached horizontal	Ambitious
Υ	Concave horizontal	Has a sense of humour
$\sqcap$	Convex horizontal	Self-protective

	Like an 'X'	Has morbid thoughts
	Flying horizontal	Protective
	Angled	Spiteful
	Short horizontal	Sarcastic
	Weak-pressure horizontal	Timid
	Horizontal to right of stem	Quick-witted
	Horizontal to left of stem	Lives in the past
	Horizontal placed high	Ambitious
	Horizontal placed low	Frustrated about their career
	Horizontal pointing down	Has a tendency to be depressed
	Long horizontal	Strong-willed
	Double horizontal	Compulsive
	Tepee stroke	Cautious
	Sword-like stroke	Impatient

U u

U	Simplified	Well-educated, balanced
U	Large	Hedonistic
V	Angular	Hard-working but can be undemonstrative
U	Long lead-in	Critical and analytical
U	Horseshoe	Controlling
U	Narrow	Inhibited
U	Loops on tops	Feigns friendliness
U	Taller second stroke	Inventive
N	Angles on lower case 'u'	Opinionated
U	Unadorned, rounded base	Passive
U	Starting stroke from lower zone	Poser!
U	Open at the base	Less than honest

V v

V	Hook on final stroke	Cutting
✓	Extended final stroke	Ambitious
V	Antler formation	Balanced
V⁻	Horizontal end stroke	Protective
U	Rounded	Kind
Y	Seagull formation	Devious
U	Looped	Secretive
X	Crossed swords	Aggression

W w

	Long end stroke	Ambitious
	Curved-in end stroke	Protective
	Rounded	Sensitive, poetic
	Narrow and tall	Shy, inhibited
	Looped	Eccentric, ostentatious
	Retraced	Inhibited, cautious
	Angle lead-in	Critical, practical
	Hook on end stroke	Vindictive
	Two 'v' shapes	Deeply eccentric, a show-off
	Thread	Versatile
	Wavy line	Artistic
	Bizarre shape	Possibly harbours erotic fantasies
	All loops	Feigns friendliness

X x

X	Simplified	Well-balanced
X	Long downward stroke	Aggressive, impatient
X	Heavy pressure	Stubborn and/or stressed
X	Light pressure	Has poor willpower
X	Tall upstroke	Very ambitious
⊃⊂	Two curves	Mathematical
⊃⊂	Overlapping curves	Family-orientated
X	Split strokes	Indecisive
∝	Like ampersand	Attached to the past

Y y

7	Like figure 7	Good concentration
4	Square	Constructive ability
Y	Excessive pressure on downstroke	Bad-tempered
ч	Short downstroke	Repressed
y	Cradling lower-zone formation	Maternal
ʏ	Long straight lower zone	Strong physical drive
ƍ	Large lower loop	Strong sexual imagination
ᶁ	Claw-like formation	Unconscious guilt
¥	Triangle in lower zone	Frustrated and angry
ʏ	Tick in lower zone	Sexually frustrated
y	Lower-zone stroke crossing middle zone	Self-indulgent
ч	Lower-zone stroke to right	Altruistic
ꙏ	Unusual lower-zone strokes	Has unusual sexual interests!
ʏ	Retraced lower zone	Sexually repressed

Z

Z	Simplified	Intelligent and down to earth
ℒ	Looped	Determined
ʒ	Curved final stroke	Easy-going
Z___	Extended final stroke	Vain and proud
Z	Ticks	Nervous
⅜	Long upward end stroke	Quick-tempered
ς	Like backward 's'	Friendly
Ʒ	Angled	Angry
ʒ	Embellished	Neurotic

Can you remember that right at the beginning of this book I asked you to write 'The quick brown fox jumps over the lazy dog'? Turn back to that now or, if you like, write it out again, and see how many individual letter shapes you can identify from the list that I have given you.

Do these traits complement everything else that you have learned about yourself so far?

Exercise 18: Letter Specifics

See how you fare pitting your wits against these conundrums.

Who is the more secretive out of these three characters?

A   *you can tell me*

B   *you can tell me*

C   *you can tell me*

The answer is B. Spot the looped ovals on the 'o' and 'a'.

What can you tell about the open ovals of the letters 'o' and 'a' in figure A?

They love to chat and are very open about themselves!

In figure C, what do you make of the triangular formation to the 'y'?

The writer is feeling frustrated and angry. Can you spot anything else about the handwriting that confirms this? Look at the end strokes and the heavy pressure . . . Yikes!

Who is the most stubborn out of these three?

A I'm not moving

B I'm not moving

C I'm not moving

It's figure A. Those long strokes staking the ground from both the 'm's and the 'g' aren't going anywhere!

Which one is most likely to have an interest in the architectural or construction industry?

Look at figure B. Those squared-off 'n's and 'm's show a love of form and construction.

What can you say about figure C based on what you've gleaned from this chapter?

The knotted oval shows secrecy and discretion, but the large cradling 'g' reveals a maternal side to the personality, while the circle above the 'i' shows a rather 'young' mentality. Remember, we can't tell the age of a writer from the handwriting . . . So maybe they are actually a teenager or maybe they just have a youthful, idealised view of the world.

WHOSE LINE IS IT ANYWAY?

Have a look at these four famous personalities below and see what you can detect from their handwriting.

This gift which we shall greatly
enjoy and appreciate.

Elizabeth R

Queen Elizabeth II

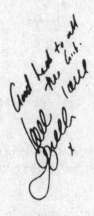

David Beckham

Open your heart ...
open your mind ...

Prince

WITH BEST
WISHES

Walt Disney

HRH Queen Elizabeth II

The Queen of England has a fluid, pleasing rhythm to her writing, with well-balanced spacing and size, but what do you make of the following letter specifics:

Rightward movement to lower-zone 'y' strokes.

Tall upper-zone loops.

High-flying 't' bars.

'g' like figure 8.

Her Royal Highness shows a strong altruistic side to her personality (note the rightward movement to lower-zone 'y' strokes) and a sense of pride (tall upper-zone loops) but also she is highly protective of others as well as herself (high-flying 't' bars). Her figure 8 'g's show that she has a quick mind and is certainly no slouch when it comes to literary and intellectual matters.

David Beckham

We know that David was an international superstar of football, but what about his off-screen personality?

David appears to have an extrovert, easy-going personality, but the handwriting also shows us that he is protective about his private life, even secretive (see the excessive looped ovals in the middle zone). The ink-filled middle-zone letters point to a love of the good things in life and an easy sensuality, but the lack of embellishment to the letter 't' and its relatively highly placed bar remind us that he is both ambitious and single-minded when it comes to his career.

Back of the net!

Prince

The late singer and performer Prince needs little introduction, but let's see what we can deduce from this sample of handwriting.

The letter 'O' with its loop within a loop shows that Prince was secretive to the point of being defensive about his personal life, despite what the childlike 'i' circle and drawn hearts may make us believe.

The concave 't' bar bears out his great sense of style and humour and the inflated 'd' loop underlines his strong emotional side.

Walt Disney

There can be few of us whose childhoods and adulthoods haven't been enriched by the work of Walt Disney. But what of the man himself? His handwriting certainly looks complex and very unique. Let's take a look at the specifics.

Walt Disney seems to have been a complex character and was probably little understood beyond his prolific and highly successful career.

The looped 'W' shows us that he was an eccentric character who could be impatient (sword-like 't' stroke). The printed 'H' with its longer second vertical stroke also shows us that he could be stubborn and liked his own way.

It is interesting to note that Walt Disney's handwriting is printed in capitals, apart from his signature. What do you think that means?

In the next chapter we are going to be looking at signatures. Walt Disney has an extremely distinctive one, so jot down what you make of it before turning the page, and then see if your opinion changes at the end of it.

Chapter 16

THE SIGNATURE

Even those of us that profess not to write by hand much any more will still be called upon to put pen to paper when signing various documents.

If, like me, you practised writing your signature as a child over and over again until you liked the look of it, then you may begin to understand what the signature might say about a writer.

Not only is it a mark of possession and of independence – this is me and it belongs to me – it is also a unique stamp of individuality.

However, as you know, handwriting can subtly or dramatically change, and even one's signature is subject to change over the years. Many years ago, I had a couple of cheques rejected because my bank didn't recognise my signature. Nowadays we are more reliant on pin numbers and other forms of identification. However, the fact remains that the signature is still a crucial part of our identity.

We have already talked about the personal pronoun revealing our perceived position in the world, but the signature shows something entirely different: how we would like to be seen by others. It is our shop window, our subconscious website.

But this is where things get interesting: the image that we portray may or may not be reflected in reality. Reality is to be found in the main text of the handwriting, and so one should always compare a signature to the main text. Is it the same or is it wildly different?

There is often only a narrow gap between truth and fiction, and for some people the truth is what they will always display. In this case you will see a signature that looks in every way – size, spacing, pressure, letter formation etc. – the same as the main body of writing.

does what it says on the tin

Timothy Normal

In this case, what you see is what you get. This person pretty much behaves in public how they would behave in private. There is little façade or artifice. How very refreshing!

Let's have a look at signatures in more detail.

Signature Larger Than Text

Let's pretend I'm really important

Charlotte Shouman

Nothing wrong with this ego! They want to be seen as more important than they really feel. They are literally bigging themselves up . . .

Signature Smaller Than Text

I'm ever so humble

Fay O'way

This writer has chosen to take a back seat, to fade into the crowd. It's possible that their self-confidence evaporates when in a room full of people. They may not want to draw attention to their insecurities.

Right-Slanted Signature With Left-Slanted Text

Look how outgoing I am

Merry Smile

It's important for this person to portray a more outgoing and friendly disposition than they actually feel. Shy within, they have a well-constructed façade of someone more self-confident.

Left-Slanted Signature With Right-Slanted Text

I need to hold back

Ant I. Shy

This is a rather rare combination . . . The writer feels that they need to hold their personality in check for some reason. A false reserve.

Vertical Signature With Right-Slanted Text

I'm as cool as a cucumber

Penny Poised

This person is emotional in private but they have chosen to portray themselves as a very upright, rather staid personality. The ultimate diplomat perhaps . . .

Upward-Sloping Signature

I love being in public

Phil Anderer

This person's self-image makes them feel energised.

Downward-Sloping Signature

my image is not so good

Iva Problem

It's hard for the writer to feel confident about their public image. What is going on in their life?

Sometimes you come across a signature in which just one of the names – given or family – slopes down. What do you think this could indicate?

I'm regretting this marriage

Mayda Mistake

The placement of the signature on the page also has significance.

Is it just creeping onto the page or making a dash for the exit?

Signature Placed on Right of Page

Just getting on with life

Victor Vital

It is very common to place a signature to the right of the page. This indicates a healthy, vital and progressive outlook to life.

Signature Placed on Left of Page

finding it hard to move forward

Irma Clinger

There is a reluctance to move forward here.

Signature Placed in Centre of Page

don't leave me out of things
C. Everything .

This writer has a need to be at the centre of all that they do and wants other people to know that they are worthy of the attention.

Do remember that all these traits can be transitory, and signature placements, although useful by comparison with text, can change with our moods, our energy levels as well as our attitude towards the recipient.

Have you ever come across a perfectly legible script in a letter and then you have no idea what the signature says? I certainly have, and often.

Illegible Signature With a Legible Script

It's of little importance who I am.

The writer certainly wants to convey their ideas and thoughts but at the same time feels a need to hide behind a wall of anonymity. Perhaps they feel unworthy of what they are writing about. They are likely to be secretive.

Occasionally you will come across a signature that looks like a hieroglyph or symbol as opposed to an actual name.

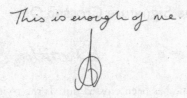

Depending on the size, formation and placement, the writer could be highly creative or highly evasive.

What do you think about the writer above?

Legible Signature With an Illegible Script

And for thinking by me

Eva Bonkers

This is far more unusual. There is a touch of eccentricity here, but it could also point to a 'skating over' of the facts of the text in question. Does the writer normally write with an illegible hand?

There are other signature anomalies . . .

Parts of Signature Differ in Size

Lucy Lastic   *Lucy Lastic.*

The writer may well harbour negative thoughts about either her given or family name. How does she feel about her family? Is she trying to diminish the importance of one part of her life perhaps?

Part or All of The Signature Crossed Out

Rhanda Bend   *Rhonda Bend*

Which bit of the name has been crossed out? Is she trying to eradicate her family name (married or otherwise), or is she harbouring hostility and bad feelings about herself? Check to see if this is normal for the writer or a transitory habit.

I have come across this often in my career and there are nearly always feelings of anger, shame or depression behind it.

Signature Circled

Sandy Bottom

We have talked about handwriting upper zones that curl back on themselves – this is another form of self-protection. The writer feels a need to keep themselves safe and even a little defensive in public. Are they a little touchy? Does it feel like walking on eggshells when dealing with them?

Full Stop at End of Signature

Ed Bugy.

The full stop should be superfluous at the end of a signature, but some people feel a need to show that this is really the end of the matter.

Line Under Signature

This writer feels important and wants to make sure everybody is aware of it.

Full Stop and Line Under Signature

Yes, you guessed it . . . This one likes the last word *and* they think they're important.

Exercise 19 : Signatures

Write out a made-up letter and sign it at the end (with your normal signature and not just the one that after reading this chapter you *wished* you had . . .).

Write down all the differences that you can see between your signature and the main body of text. What do you deduce from this? Observe whether your signature has changed over the years. If it has, why would that be?

Which of these writers has negative feelings towards their family?

A

B

C

It's B. The writer has crossed out their surname. They feel so much more comfortable alone, in their own company.

Which of the three feels very sure of themselves?

The answer is C. The full stop and underscore shows self-confidence.

Writer A has completely encircled their name. They are not at all self-confident and, for the time being at least, feel a need to defend their corner.

What does your signature say about you?

Does your signature mirror
your handwriting?

YES

YOU ARE WHAT YOU
ARE! NO FACADE
NECESSARY

NO

Is your signature a
different size from text?

YES

DO YOU FEEL A
NEED TO HIDE
AWAY OR SHOUT
YOUR MESSAGE
FROM THE ROOFTOPS
TO BE UNDERSTOOD?

NO

CHECK FOR
DIFFERENCE
IN SLANT,
POSITION, ETC?

YOU HAVE A PERSONALITY THAT FEELS
THE NEED TO PUT ON A FACADE TO
OTHERS. HAPPIER? CALMER? MORE
EXTROVERT? OR ARE YOU UNCERTAIN
ABOUT YOUR IDENTITY?

WHOSE LINE IS IT ANYWAY?

Here are some famous signatures and texts. What do you make of their similarities and differences, and what does this reveal about the writers themselves?

Happy Birthday and
'Nice Hat!'
Love from Harry

Prince Harry

raking it such a fine
visit.
Best wishes.
Catherine Middleton

The Duchess of Cambridge

Congratulations!
Best wishes,
Bill Gates

Bill Gates

Keep working Good & Playing Well

Venus Williams

Prince Harry

Prince Harry on first glance appears to have a similar signature to his text, and the upright slant, heavy pressure and tall upper zone all match.

However, do you notice that the second vertical stroke on the capital 'H' reaches right down to the lower zone? Prince Harry certainly likes to have his own way over things, and there is stubbornness here. The upright slant shows that he actually keeps his emotions, for the most part, in check, but the heavy pressure and rightward-placed signature indicate healthy vitality.

That sweeping underscore under the signature? Yes, he wants to be noticed!

The Duchess of Cambridge

Catherine Middleton really does show us a great example of a signature that matches her script. The size, speed and legibility all match. She has also placed her name bang in the middle of the page.

She knows her own mind, has a healthy ego and feels absolutely no need to put on airs and graces.

Bill Gates

Bill Gates, the well-known American entrepreneur and philanthropist, also has a matching signature. He has even lined it up perfectly with the rest of the script.

He is comfortable in his own skin and is happy to display his personality to the outer world.

Venus Williams

This tennis champion has a rather different signature to the text.

The text is legible, vertical and with a smattering of angles and arcades as connective strokes.

Venus' signature is not really legible, larger than the script and has garlanded formations with one very large sweeping arcade stroke which covers her entire name. What do you make of this?

She is certainly theatrical but is feeling a need to show her softer, more emotional side, and that sweeping covering stroke indicates that she can feel defensive at times. It's a tough business being at the top of your game . . . Do you also notice the figure 8, subconsciously drawn?

This could mean that her eyes are on the prize, or her bank balance!

Here are more famous signatures for you to analyse . . .

Je vous souhaite une bonne
santé pour 2014.

Salutations

Roger Federer

translated from
the original runes
by

J.K. Rowling

GOOD TASTE IS A GIFT
BUT BAD TASTE IS A PRIVILEGE

Kanye West

Roger Federer

This is another tennis champion, but would you be able to read his name if I hadn't told you who it was? It certainly seems as though what Federer is saying to us is more important than how he perceives himself. Those large loops and circles in his name are not evident in his main text.

He wants to be seen as both creative and emotional. The main text says that he is also determined, intuitive and uncompromising.

J.K. Rowling

This internationally famous author has a signature which is larger than her text, more rounded and with sweeping arcade strokes in the upper zone. It is rather illegible but has great form quality and a thread connection.

She has a quick mind, a huge imagination and a healthy dose of pride.

Kanye West

What do you make of this? Kanye has printed the text of this note but the signature is illegible, to the far right of the paper, shows extreme connection and there are angles amidst the thread.

Kanye may want to get his message across but he is also extremely private, doesn't suffer fools gladly and can be impatient.

Look at the little figure that he's drawn. I'm not sure if this is a 'signature' trademark but it does rather look as though it is behind bars . . .

I have said to you that a signature on its own means little, but here are three isolated signatures from individuals that have very different careers. What do you make of their public image?

Usain Bolt

Jay-Z

Rupert Murdoch

Usain Bolt

Usain may be one of the fastest runners in the world but the scored-through signature shows that even he has self-doubt. The large capitals show that, on the other hand, he wants to be noticed . . .

Jay-Z

This signature is large, with an illegible and extremely creative short form to his letters.

This singer is a real one-off – creative, sure of himself and with a wonderfully vital energy.

Rupert Murdoch

Love him or hate him, his signature shows emotion (large loops), intelligence (high form level and fast speed) and stubborn determination (long middle-zone stroke into the lower zone).

The hook at the end of the name shows how important family is to him, and that underscore shows that he knows who the boss is!

Famous signatures are relatively easy to find online. Try seeking out your favourite personalities and see if you can throw a new light onto their public persona.

Chapter 17

DANGER SIGNS

When studying graphology I was also asked to decipher the personalities of some notorious murderers throughout history. Some of the samples were very obviously screaming out their murderous tendencies at me, but others were more subtly worrying.

All of us possess angelic and devilish sides to our character depending on the circumstances that we find ourselves in. We have already touched upon a few things to be wary of in each chapter, but there are certain traits that, in combination with others, add up to a more than passing negativity. Rather, a big red flag.

I have divided up these danger signs into three categories: dishonesty and its various manifestations; violence and aggressive tendencies; and, finally, emotional instability.

Before I go any further, there are a few rules I need to repeat, as well as a couple of new ones I need to mention:

- Please don't diagnose your other half, employer or soon-to-be-ex-best friend as a psychopath or homicidal maniac! None of us are perfect or one hundred per cent honest about everything. We can all show lack of empathy, and even unkindness at times.

Always look at the handwriting as a whole, not just individual characteristics. Is this person basically happy, honest and caring, but occasionally shows signs of irritation? If so, they are unlikely to be a serial killer. If, however, you see a handwriting that shows signs of brutality, violence, emotional instability and untempered aggression, then you may need to reconsider employing them in your company, for example.

- There are graphologists who specialise in determining physical and mental illness. Please never ever do this, as you will almost certainly be wrong, and even graphologists need many years of experience before they can make any such judgement.

- Another important consideration is that substance abuse, whether it be alcohol or drugs, can show up as a danger sign. There is a big difference between someone who has had one glass of wine compared to the chronic alcoholic. Again, addiction is a large and complex subject; please do not even attempt an amateur diagnosis.

Dishonesty

If a handwriting is legible, rhythmic with an even pressure and the letters look natural without too much embellishment (as we discussed in Chapter 11, 'Form Quality'), then we see a character that is unlikely to make our blood run cold on first glance.

What about those amongst us who make a habit of deceiving, defrauding, stealing, forging or conning others? How do we spot these undesirable creatures through their handwriting? Look for a combination of several of the characteristics below to alert you.

VERY SLOW SPEED

am I sincere?

Very carefully formed letter strokes can be indicative of calculation. A lack of spontaneity could tip over into cunning.

NUMEROUS EMBELLISHMENTS

Well hello!

Too many curlicues, embellishments and other frippery can make us blind to what is going on beneath.

VERY SINUOUS BASELINE

wriggling out of things easily.

If we see an invisible baseline as an indication of our subconscious emotional boundary, then this could be perceived as a lack of control.

ILLEGIBILITY

Can't make head nor tails of this

Illegibility takes many forms (over-coiling, indistinct letter formations, etc.) but chronic illegibility may be a sign of an unwillingness to communicate in a straightforward manner.

COILED AND TIGHTLY KNOTTED OVALS

not telling you anything

A plethora of coiled and knotted ovals denotes extreme secrecy. What are they trying to hide?

VERY LIGHT PRESSURE

Easily led

Pressure that is very light and not caused by physical weakness can be a sign of weak willpower. It may seem harsh to say so, but this person could be easily led by others into a life of crime.

THREADS WITHIN WORDS

what am I hiding?

Speed is generally a good thing, but not if it is achieved by just pulling out the middle of every word into a formless thread. If there are other indications, then this writer could be more than willing to cover up what's important.

RIGID BASELINES

I'm thinking very carefully

Along with slow speed, an overly rigid baseline is a sign of calculation. The writer wants to be seen to fit in with society a little bit too much. Of course, they could simply be a people pleaser, but on the other hand there may be further signs of premeditation and conniving tendencies.

EXTREME ARCADING

I love hiding

Although arcade formations are used by more traditional writers, their use also betrays a less emotional side. Too much arcading could be indicative of a lack of empathy, which of course can mean a less than honest nature.

RETRACING/RETOUCHING

hesitation and playing for time

Retracing in any zone indicates tension, but excessive retracing, especially in the upper zone, as well as a constant retouching of letters are danger signs: indicative of a writer's need to make his or her reality match with others, relentless inner tension and uncontrolled nervousness. Why would this be?

OVERLY INFLATED UPPER ZONE

let me tell you a story

Huge swollen upper loops can be a sign of a fantastical imagination or, in the extreme, a pathological liar.

OVERLY INFLATED LOWER ZONE

I want what you have always

If there are big lower-zone loops, this can be an indication of greed and even a need for these desires to be met at any cost.

ESSENTIAL BITS OF LETTERS OR WORDS OMITTED

I dont want you to know

This is an unusual sign, but if a writer consistently leaves out essential bits of the letters and even words, once again they may well be trying to evade the real truth of the matter.

VERY TALL CAPITALS

Im A God!

This is a sign of an arrogant nature and a need to be something they're not.

SHARK'S TOOTH FORMATION

Wolf in sheeps clothing

Some covering strokes actually look like sharks' teeth. This person is capable of covering up all manner of behaviour. At its worst it could indicate sharp practice.

OVALS OPEN AT BASE

doing my own thing

Open ovals at the top are very common and can indicate a chatty nature, but open at the bottom is harder to achieve and thankfully less common. This writer is unlikely to be concerned with convention or indeed what others think of them. This sort of attitude could also lead to a disregard for normal standards of honesty.

VERY FLAMBOYANT SIGNATURE

An overly flamboyant or ridiculously embellished signature should ring a large alarm bell – what character are they trying to act out? The swindler, perhaps, or the seducer?

Always look at contrasting signatures and scripts. If the difference is very marked, then so is the difference between reality and perception.

Violence and Aggressive Tendencies

Violence tends not to be transitory but a much more fixed and dangerous sign of lack of control.

VERY HEAVY PRESSURE

Can't control my emotions

Very heavy pressure can be an indication of intense emotions that the writer has difficulty in controlling.

VARIABLE PRESSURE

Volatile feelings

As above, but the erratic nature of the emotions can present itself as dangerous volatility.

PASTY AND SMEARED LETTER FORMATIONS

Dangerous

Sometimes the writing is so thickly placed on the paper that the writing looks 'pasty' and even smeary. This is a big red flag for anger, aggression and even violence – but, as always, do look out for more than this one sign.

HEAVY DOWNWARD-FACING 'T' BARS

getting my own way

The writer has to have their own way, and this may be a sign of aggression.

CLUB-ENDED 'T' BARS

get out!

This 't' bar isn't just short but thick and clubbed. An angry sign . . .

DAGGER-SHAPED 'T' BARS

definitely get out

Never ignore the dagger-shaped 't' bar – these slashing strokes mean business.

CLUBBED DOWNWARD ENDINGS

cruelty every day

As above, these clubbed strokes, which look as though they have been prematurely and abruptly ended with a heavy stroke, are yet another pointer towards a stubborn, but – in its worst form – hostile and aggressive nature.

LONG STICK FIGURES IN LOWER ZONE

frustrated every day – keep away!

Very long lower-zone strokes that look unfinished and out of sync with the rest of the writing can mean frustration and physical disturbance. This unenviable trait can tip over into cutting sarcasm, but can also reveal a problem with anger management.

MISPLACED CAPITAL LETTERS

breaking bAd.

Capital letters placed in the middle of a word not only look very out of place, but also show us a writer that can be impulsive, overly emotional and capable of losing their temper *very* quickly.

INK-FILLED OVALS

hot temper

A bit like heavy-pressured or pasty handwriting, if the small ovals in middle-zone letters have been filled in with ink then look for a verbal temper . . .

STABS IN OVALS

losing temper easily

Stab-like markings or ticks within ovals are an example of an extreme temper or lack of emotional control.

EXTREME ANGULARITY

I have a short fuse !

Just the look of this is painful and aggressive. Extreme angularity is a critical and aggressive sign – a bit like barbed wire personified.

X-LIKE FORMATIONS

not feeling great

A collection of X-like formations unnecessarily placed can divulge an obsession with death and endings. This can be for a number of reasons, but is also seen in more dangerous criminals and killers than the average Jo or Joe!

Emotional Instability

We have covered many danger signs already, with many of them indicating emotional instability, but there are a few other signs that point towards an unbalanced state of mind.

Everybody goes through times in life when they feel miserable, out of sorts and lacking in direction. Some people, however, show chronic signs of instability, and when several of these crop up in the same handwriting it is impossible to ignore.

UNRHYTHMIC WRITING

When writing lacks harmony and rhythm and there are a large number of irregularities, this points to someone who is out of kilter with their environment. Further examination of the writing will help you work out what form this can take. The more irregularities, both big and small, in the writing, the greater the emotional instability.

ERRATIC SIZE

An imbalance in the size of letters and even within the three zones indicates the erratic way that the writer approaches life. This makes for uncertain responses towards others.

ERRATIC SPEED

Most of us have a fairly steady writing speed, whether quick or slow. If, however, you come across speed that fluctuates hugely between the two, then this is another indication of a stop-start emotional state. The writer experiences anxiety and their behaviour is unlikely to be stable.

ERRATIC SPACING

Sha ll | come or shal | lg o?

If you recall, spacing shows us how we relate to the world around us. Most writing has a uniformity that makes it easy to analyse. Sometimes a script defies easy diagnosis – a large discrepancy in spacing between letters, words and even lines indicates uneven social attitudes.

INFLATED MIDDLE ZONE

it's all about me...me...me

Children often write with large middle zones because they haven't yet learned to consider others, but in an adult hand this can indicate not only immaturity, but a self-obsessed individual.

ERRATIC SLANT

blow hot and cold

Slant shows us the emotional nature of the writer – erratic slants show us a versatility of emotions, but also an inability to be even-tempered.

EXTREMELY INCLINED SLANT

So excited about everything!

An extreme right slant indicates a highly emotional and impulsive individual.

EXTREMELY RECLINED SLANT

must be on my own for a while.

An extreme left slant (in a right-handed writing) shows a repressed and perhaps even evasive character.

CROWDED/TANGLED LINES

can't see the trees.

When the letters, words and the lines are tangled like a coil of wires we can see a real confusion of thoughts and emotions.

UNEVEN OR NO MARGINS

He or she literally has no boundaries socially and may actually harbour a secret fear or loathing of being on their own.

HUGE WRITING

Taking my clothes off in public

Not just large writing, but enormous writing that leaps off the page to bite you can point to a writer that really has no boundaries or sensitivity towards their environment.

TINY WRITING

never taking them off…

Teeny-tiny writing that you almost need a microscope to read shows an introverted and inhibited writer, and this could result in a lack of ability to relate successfully to others.

VERY NARROW LETTER FORMATIONS

I'm very uptight

Extremely narrow letters are another red flag signalling inhibition, self-consciousness and perhaps a self-critical nature.

DISTORTED LOOPS

little bit odd

Distorted and bent or broken loops in any zone will indicate unusual emotional responses.

EXTREMELY DISCONNECTED OR PRINTED WRITING

I doNT LIKE YOU.

In old films, anonymous letters or blackmail notes would be pasted onto the page from cut-out letters from magazines. As well as preserving the anonymity of the sender, there was an intrinsically threatening look to this disjointed, self-conscious communication. In much the same way, writing that has been totally disjointed or printed in capitals can look equally menacing.

OVERLY EMBELLISHED PERSONAL PRONOUN

I love myself.

This writer is self-obsessed and spends far longer not only writing their personal pronoun but also thinking about themselves rather than others.

LONG STROKES THROUGH SIGNATURE

Irma Failure

This shows poor self-image, particularly if there are other indications in the handwriting itself.

A SPECIAL NOTE ABOUT THE 'FELON'S CLAW'

I really fancy you.

There is one graphological indication which is easy to spot and easy to interpret because it looks like a sharp claw. The usual lower-zone stroke turns straight away from the vertical to the arch instead of going into a loop, hence the claw comparison.

This is a red flag to deception. If there are other signs confirming this, you could be dealing with someone who may appear to be your best friend or lover but who can turn against you as quickly as he or she turned against the natural flow of the writing.

The more pronounced the claw, the more pronounced the guilt.

I'm not going to ask you to look at your own handwriting to look for danger signs as hopefully there aren't any. However, have a look at these samples and see how many red flags you can find and what they might mean.

A   I would very much LOVE to
      see you

B   Let's meet up...

C   see me soon

Answer

A

Embellished personal pronoun.
Erratic slant.
Clubbed lower-zone endings.
Threading in middle of word.
Printed letters.
Long, stabbing horizontal strokes.
Filled-in ovals.
Felon's claw.
Narrow middle-zone 'u'.

He or she shows signs of self-obsession, secrecy, dishonesty, cruelty . . . I could go on. I think there are probably enough red flags with this one to cast doubt on any ordinary relationship!

B

Overly rigid baseline.
Large middle zone.
Overly arcaded connections.
Open oval at bottom.

There may not be as many red flags as A, but there are still enough here to indicate someone who feels a need to present a false impression to the world.

C

Excessive angular formations.
Long, dagger-like stroke into lower zone.

I certainly wouldn't wish to see this writer again soon, as there is more than one sign of aggression in their handwriting.

WHICH OF THESE WRITERS APPEARS TO BE THE MORE HOT-TEMPERED?

A *I'll look after you.*

B *I'll look after you.*

I would be more inclined to spend time with writer A, wouldn't you? B has a nasty temper.

WHICH OF THESE WRITERS APPEARS MORE HONEST?

A *great with money*

B *great with money*

B is the more obviously honest out of these two writers.

WHICH OF THESE WRITERS HAS MORE STABLE EMOTIONS?

A   Honestly I'm fine

B   Honestly Im Fine

Writer A is the one who is more likely to be telling the truth about their state of mind.

WHOSE LINE IS IT ANYWAY?

Here are four individuals who have made it into the public eye – not always in a good way . . .

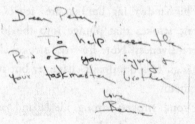

Dear Peter,
To help ease the
Pain of your injury &
your taskmaster brother
love
Bernie

Bernie Madoff

TO PATRICK
LOVE,
Nancy Vicious
Sid Vicious

Sid and Nancy Vicious

See, we used to have satellite dishes and could get cable type programs (A s.i.la. church donated this system.) . . . but the clowns that ran this place decided we were living it up too much, so disconnected them and took them out. I couldn't even see this report, if I agreed to help you with it.

Bobby Jo Long

Can you spot the traits that may have alarmed graphologists?

Bernie Madoff

Bernie Madoff is an American fraudster who set up a Ponzi scheme that robbed hundreds of their life savings. There will be many things that you can analyse from this sample of his handwriting, but here are a few of the negatives.

Long middle-zone strokes that plunge into the lower zone: extreme restlessness and defensiveness. Note how the strokes slash to the right of the page. This is a sign of a dominant character but one that is working against the environment.

Very tall upper-zone strokes: strong ideals and aspirations but not necessarily in line with reality or legality.

Ink-filled and tightly looped ovals: high degree of secrecy and habitual concealing of facts. Highly ambitious.

Erratic printing mixed with connected letters: the writer shows inconsistency in thinking processes.

Erratic size of middle-zone letters: inconsistency of reactions make this trait a pointer for instability.

What else can you deduce from the handwriting? What do you make of the large arcaded 'f', for example?

Sid and Nancy Vicious

The late Sid Vicious, the most infamous member of the Sex Pistols, and his girlfriend Nancy, led brief and chaotic lives, and were known for their erratic behaviour. What danger signs can you make out from this brief note?

Retraced capital: a lapse of concentration but also the heavy pressure indicates an obsessional individual who lacks willpower and restraint.

Erratic printing mixed with connected letters: inconsistent thought processes.

Erratic pressure: evasive and paranoid behaviour trait.

What do you make of Sid's signature? Have a look at those circle 'i' dots.

Despite the emotionally disturbed character traits there is also a childlike need for attention.

Bobby Jo Long

Robert Long is a mass murderer and rapist who committed his crimes in the 1980s. What danger signs are the first to leap off the page?

Extremely long and heavy 't' bars: the 't' bars dominate this sample and indicate persistence to the point of dangerous obsession, while the heavy pressure shows that energy could be directed into aggression or even violence.

Strongly angular connection and strokes: there is a lack of empathy and excess of control and manipulation.

Rigidity of rightward slant: strong level of neurosis.

Does this writing frighten you just by looking at it?

Chapter 18

PUTTING IT ALL TOGETHER

Hopefully by this point you have been looking at your own and other people's handwriting in quite a new way, and feel you understand graphology a bit better.

Let's put your new-found knowledge to the test. Overleaf is a sample of handwriting for you to have a look at, as well as a checklist of traits that we have covered to help you come to your conclusions. You will find my own observations on p. 277.

Always be tactful and kind and respect privacy when commenting on someone's handwriting. Never be tempted to talk about what you have deduced from friends and family's handwriting without their permission, and remember – you are not a professional graphologist and your analyses should be illuminating and fun! Never say things that would hurt others.

Before consulting the checklist, just look at the writing, see what jumps out at you and get a feel for your initial impressions. In time you will see that you were probably right.

Sample for Analysis

This writer is a 60-year-old right-handed female called Audrey. Use the checklist below to draw your conclusions. Write them on a separate sheet before looking at my own observations.

THE ZONES

What is Audrey's main focus in life, would you say? What do her upper, middle and lower zones say about her?

SLANT

How does Audrey express emotion?

BASELINE

How flexible is Audrey?

PRESSURE

How much energy does Audrey have?

SIZE

How does Audrey project herself to the wider world?

SPACING

How does Audrey relate to others? Look at the spacing within and between words, and between lines too. Look at the margins as well.

SPEED

How fast are Audrey's thought processes?

CONNECTING STROKES

Angles, arcades, threads or garlands? How does Audrey choose to project her character traits?

FORM QUALITY

How much harmony does Audrey display? Is there rhythm or chaos in her life?

LEAD-IN AND END STROKES

How much does Audrey prepare before she acts and how easily does she move on?

CONNECTION AND DISCONNECTION

How does Audrey compile her thoughts? Is she logical or intuitive?

PERSONAL PRONOUN

How does Audrey view herself?

SIGNATURE

How does Audrey want others to view her?

INDIVIDUAL LETTER FORMATIONS

Note down any peculiar or interesting letter shapes that you have learned about and jot down their meaning.

DANGER SIGNS

Are there any big red flags to note?

Observations – My Analysis

These are the notes I made at first glance when looking at Audrey's writing:

Moderate Left Slant – some inner withdrawal, attachment to the past, maybe to a mother figure. Some repression and fear of change and possibly of the future.

Thread connecting strokes – quick-minded, curious about the world.

Garlanded and arcaded 'm' and 'n' with some threaded 'm' and 'n' strokes – friendly but has short attention span.

Long 't' bars but often to the left of 't' bar – energy and vigour, but relates to the past more than the future.

This is what I jotted down from looking at the writing in more detail.

THE ZONES

Upper zone

Mainly stick figure. Average to tall in height.

Practical and independent thinker. Enjoys facts, not theory. Healthy mental processes.

Middle zone

Fluctuation in size from average to very small. Some letters illegible.

Some mood instability noted. Emotional volatility. Inconsistency of reaction.

Lower zone

Unembellished stick figure. Size – average to stunted.

Practical, can be unemotional. Good at planning. Veers between physical energy and physical frustration.

I also noticed that the upper zone is slightly taller than the lower zone is long. This means she can be idealistic. Her ego appears healthy but Audrey can suffer from feelings of inferiority.

SLANT

Slight left slant.

There is a healthy emotional front but partly superficial. Audrey represses true feelings due to fear of the unknown. Holding back of emotions.

BASELINE

Baseline is fairly rigid.

Fear of losing control and some inhibition. Prefers planning to spontaneity.

PRESSURE

Handwriting pressure is normal to average.

Healthy vitality.

SIZE

Overall size is average but with variable individual letter sizes.

Appears conventional and adaptable but can be indecisive and moody, while charming at the same time.

SPACING

Within words – widely spaced.

Healthy social interaction with others. Some narrow letters, however, show that feelings can be more cautious and measured.

Between words – average.

Healthy outlook towards society in general.

Between lines – good spacing, no tangling.

Social flexibility.

Margins – widening left margin.

Optimistic and impatient.

SPEED

Generally fast speed but slight left slant and left-placed 't' bars slow speed down somewhat.

Fairly quick-thinking processes. Healthy maturity and creativity.

CONNECTING STROKES

Thread connectors with weak garland 'm' and 'n' formations.

Fast mind but uses intuition more than logic. Creative in her own way. Can be unpredictable and a little secretive. Charming and friendly to the outside world. Some illegibility indicates covering up of insecurities by evasiveness.

FORM QUALITY

Form quality is compromised by signs of neglect, i.e. excessive threading and illegibility and missing out of essential letter parts. However, some rhythm is still achieved.

Audrey shows purpose and maturity but can be impatient and easily distracted. Prone to worry and depression at times.

LEAD-IN AND END STROKES

Lead-in strokes – absent.

Decisive and quick-minded.

End strokes – very short.

Self-sufficient. Can be frugal.

CONNECTION AND DISCONNECTION

Mainly connected, with some false connections, i.e. she takes her pen off paper but letters look connected.

Spontaneity indicated but not obsessive. Good organisational skills. Practical and realistic.

PERSONAL PRONOUN

Simple stroke.

Independent and lack of vanity.

SIGNATURE

Placed in centre of page. Similar in size and formation to main text.

Audrey, although not exhibiting a façade, has a healthy ego.

INDIVIDUAL LETTER FORMATIONS

Letters of note include:

a – Some open ovals.
Talkative.

E – Greek form of capital.
Cultured.

f – Curved in 'f' stroke. Some missing 'f' horizontals.
Defensive and can be less than transparent at times.

g – Simplified letter formation.
Quickness of mind but some physical repression.

h – No loop.
Head rules heart.

i – Above stem.
Meticulous nature.

I – Simplified.
Self-reliant.

m – Angled and flat-topped.
Efficient and practical. Some fleeting aggression.

n – Narrow garland formation with some thready indistinct 'n' shapes.
Charming, but skating over details.

r – Short simplified stroke.
Quick mind.

t – Some long 't' bars, some upward rising 't' bars and some placed to left of stem.

Combination of indecision, enthusiasm and energy. Combination of sharply angled and curved 't' bar strokes mean erratic energy levels. Some aggression.

u – Simplified strokes and missing parts of letter.
Avoidance of important issues but versatility.

W – Backward-facing final stroke on both capitals and small 'w'. Rounded formation.
Sensitivity and self-protection.

y – Thready middle-zone formation with simplified lower zone.
Poor attention to detail, speedy thought processes.

DANGER SIGNS

Few danger signs. Evidence of the following:

Variation of letter size.
Can be inconsistent in dealings with others.

Some illegibility.
Finds it difficult to communicate with others. Hiding true feelings.

Inconsistent threading.
Worry and anxiety.

Angled 't' bars.
Can have a short temper.

Inconsistency of lower-zone length.
Inconsistent energy (can be a very transitory trait).

Finally, here is my full interpretation of Audrey's sample:
'The writer is independent and self-reliant. She has traits that indicate

good organisational and practical skills but there is also evidence of creativity and a speedy original mind.

Her intellect can be hampered by self-doubt and fear of the unknown. She comes across as sociable and friendly but there is repression of true feelings and she is more attached to the past than forward-thinking. She can cling to outmoded ideals.

Physical energy is healthy for her age but she can also feel physically frustrated at times. At the time of writing, she was enthusiastic and upbeat.

She can be a worrier and finds it difficult to express her feelings of anxiety and dark thoughts; at times this comes across as moodiness and inconsistency of emotional reactions, which can confuse others.

However, she is socially adaptable and has a charm and a broad-minded attitude which is likely to attract a wide range of friends and associates.

She has a tendency to get bored easily and dislikes getting bogged down with detail. Conservative and largely conventional by nature, her head rules her heart. Her responses to others will be cautious and measured but she can also show impatience.

To sum up: she is a practical and cautious individual on one level but with a quick and impatient mind. Friendly and charming, she possesses a sociable disposition and a healthy vitality. There is some intellectual repression and an inability to see her true worth.

How did your analysis compare to mine?

Now you are ready to analyse other handwritings and soon you will not even need the checklist above to help you.

Have you tried a full analysis of your own handwriting yet?

Chapter 19

COMPATIBILITY

I am often asked whether someone's other half is right for them.

As we have been seeing, graphology can provide a wonderful understanding of a person's character, but we cannot quantify the special something that makes two people click – sexual and emotional chemistry is incredibly individual as well as subject to change. However, it is possible to ascertain a level of romantic compatibility as well as discord in two people thanks to handwriting analysis, as you will see below.

It is the same in business: we all want to find the perfect match of people to create the best team. I work frequently with companies to help them choose the right individual for a certain position, as well as helping them to restructure the company so that they are making the best of what they've got. Is this person right for their new role? Should that colleague get a promotion, for example?

After an initial job interview, a shortlist is usually drawn up of candidates who have the qualities that are needed for the job. But then what? How do you narrow the choice further?

Interviews are crucial to gauge how well someone will fit in as well as to see how an individual acts under stress. The trouble is that we often 'act' under stress and can give a false positive or negative impression in that situation. Handwriting analysis can be a really useful way of revealing what lies beneath the firm handshake in the interview (I should make it clear that I do not believe that anyone should be hired or fired on the *sole* basis of a graphological analysis).

Graphology can help by pinpointing certain qualities that don't necessarily show up on a CV or at an interview.

Let's look at personal relationships in the first instance, and then move on to professional ones.

Personal Relationships

If you are in a relationship, start by writing a few sentences in the space below and then ask your other half to write a few lines directly underneath.

....

....

....

....

....

....

....

....

What can you make of the two handwriting samples? Can you see obvious factors that could spell a mismatch? What have you noticed intuitively? Do the samples 'look' right together?

Then compare them again at the end of this section and see if you change your mind.

Here are a few factors that I think are important when considering compatibility with a significant other. I have concentrated on the mismatches, but feel free to disagree with me if you are hugely attracted to your glaring opposite. Compatibility isn't only about matching up similar, like-for-like personality traits – sometimes contrasting personalities fit together well, each partner offering something that the other lacks and vice versa.

SENSE OF HUMOUR

I take it you both have one, but do they match? A childish slapstick guffaw may grate with a dry, acerbic sense of sarcasm for instance.

A   Slap and tickle!

B   most drole

Writer A shows earthy roundness to the writing, with a teenage-style circle above the 'i' dot and a long sensual lower zone. B, conversely, has a slow, considered hand, a long, cutting 't' bar and an altogether more sophisticated style.

INTELLECTUAL INTERESTS

These can take many forms, and are not necessarily related to intelligence. But if one of you reads Proust as a bit of bedtime light reading and the other remains glued to the soap operas on TV, then you may soon tire of each other.

A   I simply adore War and Peace

B   Turn the telly on love...

Writer A has a high form level, regularity of size, spacing and speed in their writing, and the personal pronoun and arched 'd' suggest a love of culture.

B is possibly great fun but has a lower form level and a larger middle zone. The upper zone is short, which may point to the type of person that enjoys more immediate gratification and fewer highbrow pursuits.

SOCIABILITY

If one half of a couple likes going to bed at 6 p.m. and loathes parties and the other half is a huge party animal, then apart from never seeing each other, intimacy is likely to be compromised!

A   *I love a great party*

B   Bed at sundown for me.

Writer A has garland connectors, a right slant and small spaces between words – all signs of sociability. B is much drier – upright slant, wider spacing and disconnected letters. He or she is not the biggest partygoer, and could actually be a party pooper.

SENSUALITY AND SEX DRIVE

A tricky subject because, as we know, this is one area in life that is apt to go up and down.

However, a sensual beast may not want to live a monastic life.

Fireworks, or a damp squib of a match in the bedroom?

A *I could go on and on all night*

B *Night night...*

Writer A has great long lower zones, heavy pressure, filled-in ovals and the long 't' bar of stamina. B, on the other hand, has a lighter pressure, little or no lower zone and an upright slant. Put the kettle on, will you?

AMBITION AND DRIVE

Some compatibility here is important because none of us like to be considered lazy when, in fact, we are perhaps not as power crazy or ambitious as our other half, who would, for example, rather be the main breadwinner in the house. In this situation, a combination of the two may very well work.

A *I put work first*

B *I love my home*

Spot the angular connection strokes of A and their aggressive and determined 't' bars. Compare them to the more rounded strokes of B and the garlanded strokes. These point to a less ambitious, but certainly not lazy writer.

SPIRITUALITY

Do you believe in a higher being? Perhaps you have a strong faith and spirituality. If so, would you feel comfortable with a partner who had no faith, little interest in spiritual matters and was more comfortable with the material side of life?

A | Worship every day

B | I believe in myself!

Notice the tall upper zone in sample A, as opposed to the larger middle zone in sample B. Writer A has a strong spirituality which contrasts with B's more egocentric writing.

GENEROSITY

The sharing of material goods can fluctuate with income and circumstances, but the ability to share time and love tends to be a bit more of a permanent trait.

A have it all!

B just a bit.

Look at A's large overall size, the garland strokes and the wide ovals. Here we have generosity of spirit and a love of life compared to the more frugal strokes of B. No stroke is wasted or superfluous. It just looks . . . well . . . a little tight.

FAITHFULNESS

I can hear the can of worms being opened here . . .

We have all entered into relationships that we assumed were exclusive only to discover that there was a veritable harem in the wings . . . no? Just me, then!

An open relationship can suit many couples, but what should you look out for if that is far from right for you, and you want loyalty and the sort of man or woman that only has eyes for you?

A *Love every one of them*

B *just me please!*

Writer A has all the markings of an individual that likes to make an impression on a wide range of people. They are secretive about their own personal life (coiled ovals) and may not be all that they seem to be (over-embellishment). Alongside those traits are a very strong sex drive and need for excitement (long lower zone and heavy pressure).

B shows signs of being a more conventional and loyal partner, with closed but not looped ovals, regularity and balance between the zones.

CREATIVITY

A *I love detail.*

B *What detail?*

This should be rather obvious. Writer A could be an accountant in this instance (yes, some accountants can be creative): spot the careful, slow writing and the attention to detail in the carefully crossed 't' bars and 'i' dots.

B, on the other hand, has plenty of thready, speedy writing and unusual letter formations which point to a more creative mind.

If you aren't in a relationship then you can use this to have a heads-up to finding your perfect match. It may not be very romantic, however, to demand a handwriting sample on or before the first date, then make a bolt for the nearest exit if you aren't obviously compatible. On the other hand, why waste time . . .

If you're already in a relationship, please don't stop there – make a list of other qualities that you find important in your other half. Can you see these qualities in his or her writing? Does comparing their handwriting to yours help you see whether you are compromising your needs and wants?

Professional Relationships

A lot of the same traits we've seen in personal relationships are significant in the workplace but there are other more specific details to take into consideration when you want to build a fully rounded and efficient team.

The following samples show examples of traits that are often needed in the workplace, irrespective of the type of work involved. Remember that a team may require a selection of different qualities in their employees – sometimes it is useful to build a team around a number of character types such as the intuitive, the logical, the creative, the practical, etc. – but too much of a contrast and there will be clashes in the office.

Once again, add your own traits to this list. Look at your colleagues' handwriting and compare – does your relationship with them match up with the graphological conclusions? Is there tension or harmony in the workplace?

SELF-CONFIDENCE

It really doesn't matter what your job is, but if one of the team has low self-esteem and lack of confidence then this could have a negative effect throughout the workplace.

A   *I have what it takes*

B   *I'm not sure that I do*

Writer A has large writing, a confident personal pronoun and a slight right slant. Those long 't' bars exude willpower and confidence. B has a tiny personal pronoun, small overall size and large spaces between the words. It's almost like they are isolating themselves through lack of self-esteem.

HONESTY

We all want to surround ourselves with honest people, and certainly a less than honest co-worker is likely to come to blows with the rest of the team when their underhand ways are revealed.

A   *You can trust me.*

B   *you can trust me*

Writer A displays several traits of someone who is far from open. Closely tied ovals, retraced letter strokes and a rigid baseline could spell trouble for the open communicator that we see in figure B.

ENERGY

Not all jobs entail a five-mile run every morning, but most employers are going to want to see reasonable energy levels and stamina whatever the age of the candidate. Poor timekeeping is unlikely to impress the line manager and would certainly cause irritation with fellow employees.

A   *I love getting up early*

B   *I love staying in bed*

Writer A's healthy pressure, long lower zones and right slant show normal, healthy energy levels, but B has much lighter pressure, short and weak lower-zone strokes and an unstable slant. These two are unlikely to work successfully together.

FRIENDLINESS

This may seem a little glib, but there is nothing more likely to cause a bad atmosphere in the work place than a grouchy, bad-tempered individual. We can't be happy all the time, but negativity can soon spread with ill-tempered behaviour.

A   *I'm having a bad day*

B   *I can just get on with things!*

Writer A oozes bad temper! The sharp-angled strokes, angular lower zones, heavy pressure and ticks spell irritability; whereas B has more rounded connection strokes, lighter pressure and can take things in their stride.

COOPERATION

Are you happy to roll up your sleeves and get stuck in when the boss asks, or are you adamantly self-centred?

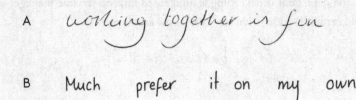

A *working together is fun*

B Much prefer it on my own

Writer A has balance between the zones, normal spacing between letters and words, and a cradling lower zone which suggests a real desire to help and nurture others; whereas B spaces their words very far apart and the letters are more upright, less emotional and far more independent of each other. This isn't all bad, because out of the two B is better at working on their own, but it is a total mismatch if they have to collaborate closely with A.

DRIVE

Sometimes companies look to employ a real 'go-getter' – someone who will stop at little to get the work done.

A *I'd like to sell you this*

B *or this might be nice...*

Writers A and B should certainly not be selling the same product, and certainly not as a duo. Writer A shows determination in the long 't' bar, a defiant enlarged letter 'k' and a strong pressure that exudes determination. B would still be taking their coat off and making a cup of tea while A secures their tenth deal of the day . . .

CONVENTIONALITY

Conventionality? Do we want that in our fellow workers? Well, we may do if the particular company and the work environment in question is fairly traditional.

A   *This is hilarious!*

B   *is it though?*

Writer A has the classic signs of eccentricity, which is surely going to narrow down his chances of getting on with the average person. The curlicues and the unnecessary strokes, as well as a plethora of exclamation marks, will soon grate on B – look at their regular spacing and size as well as rigid baseline.

INTELLIGENCE

Is the candidate someone quick to grasp new concepts? Not every job entails a high IQ, but a very slow learner may become the difference between profit or loss for a company, and would be unlikely to fit in amongst a group of fast-thinking City types, for example.

A   *This is easy for me.*

B   *can't fathom out what*

Writer A has a quick speed, tall upper zone and a high form level against B's slower hand, prominent middle zone and form level brought down a notch or two by an overly rigid, conventional handwriting.

PUNCTUALITY

This should go without saying: an employee who is late for work and meetings is unlikely to be reliable on other levels, and not a good match for a target- and deadline-based organisation.

A   *there is no rush*

B   *Always on time.*

Writer A may be congenial, but those long start and end strokes and unevenly sized letters point to someone who takes their time both getting started and moving on. They are unlikely to see the point of other people's deadlines. B has no end or start strokes and the evenness of the writing makes them reliable. This is someone who takes their duties seriously.

ATTENTION TO DETAIL

This is a trait that is likely to go hand in hand with punctuality. Some jobs depend upon it: finance (hopefully), bomb disposal (again, hopefully), surgery (ditto!), while other professions such as advertising require more creativity.

A   *crossing the 't's and dotting the 'i's.*

B   *Whatever it takes*

Writer A is going to find B highly creative but ineffectual in the financial firm that they both work in. B is going to get more than frustrated with A's insistence on getting things 'just right'.

LOGIC

Are you looking for a logical planner or an intuitive kind of person? Both are valid for different roles in life, but it's a good idea to know who is going to be the best fit for you and your business.

A   *one step at a time*

B   *I have a feeling*

Writer A's handwriting exudes logical planning: joined up and well balanced, it is really the polar opposite of the much more intuitive and mentally creative B.

DISCRETION

A   *my lips are sealed.*

B   *What secret?*

This surely is a trait that we should all be looking for in ourselves, but also those we work with (unless perhaps you are a town crier).

You will have spotted the tightly closed ovals of A, but have you seen the open oval of B? A sure sign they like to gossip . . .

LEADERSHIP QUALITIES

So you are looking to be happy in a job but you're not quite sure about your manager. Or perhaps you are employing a junior and certainly don't want them taking charge around the office in their first week.

A *happy to fit in*

B *I'm the boss*

Writer A is indeed happy to fit in and to slowly rise to the top: good form quality, even spacing and so on. B, however, is already showing leadership traits: tall and proud personal pronoun, firm pressure, angular strokes, sharp-angled downward stroke of small letter 's'. This person is unlikely to be happy sweeping the floor and making the tea. At least, not for long.

Exercise 20: Compatibility

Which handwriting traits should we be looking out for when we search for a partner? Let's have a look at the personal relationship compatibility first and see what things can alert us to a higher-than-average happiness quota or misery markers to avoid.

Here are three couples in relationships. Which one is most likely to get on beyond the honeymoon period?

A1   *we do everything together*

A2   *Yes we do!*

B1   *I really love her.*

B2   *I love her too*

C1   *we tend to argue*

C2   *gets on my nerves!*

At first glance none of the couples appear to have much in common, but couple B is likely to get into trouble early on. B1 is all middle zone – self-centred despite the proclamation of love, but B2 is more cerebral (look at the tall upper-zone and the determined 't' stroke.) They would tire of each other

The other two couples may not be perfect pairs, but they have enough similarities in areas that really matter – size and slant. Nothing is certain, but they could be in for the long haul.

How about these three couples who may go into business together. Winners or losers?

A1 *welcome to the firm*

A2 *thanks a lot*

B1 *Lets work together*

B2 *Yes lets.*

C1 *This is my business.*

C2 *thats fine.*

Once again, they all show different traits, both good and bad, but couple A has quite a serious compatibility issue. Can you spot it? A1 is incredibly secretive to the point of paranoia (tightly closed and double-looped ovals). A2, on the other hand, loves to talk and give everything away (wide, open ovals and wide spacing).

The other two pairs share traits that would make them more equal partners. Can you name them?

WHOSE LINE IS IT ANYWAY?

Here are three well-known couples who so far have stayed the course of true love. Can you see why?

letter comes with my thoughts
my condolences,

William [signature]

taking it such a fina
visit.

Best wishes,

Catherine Middleton [signature]

The Duke and Duchess of Cambridge

Jen'fo

Kim Kardashian [signature]

GOOD TASTE IS A GIFT
BUT BAD TASTE IS A PRIVILEGE

[Kanye signature]

Kim and Kanye

the guethers
See you soon

[David signature]
x

thank you for
your support!

Best Wishes.
Victoria [signature]
+

David and Victoria Beckham

The Duke and Duchess of Cambridge

The Duke and Duchess of Cambridge, although not strikingly similar personalities, have complementary handwritings.

Catherine's handwriting shows a sociable and outgoing nature, but one that enjoys her privacy. Note the right slant, small spaces between the words and tightly closed ovals. She has a good balance between the three zones and has a versatile personality.

William's handwriting is smaller, with larger spaces between the words, but he too enjoys his privacy, when he can get it. Those long lower zones that pull to the right match his wife's hard-working and energetic attitude to life. He is the more sensitive of the two and he would appreciate her balanced, sensible and nurturing nature.

Kim and Kanye

In these two samples we can see more of an obvious match. Both have chosen the dense sensuality of a thick nib which shows their well-matched vitality and libido. Kanye's printing shows a need to be understood and noticed, which is matched by Kim's large-sized writing and strong downward strokes of the letter 'k'.

They are both stubborn and like to have their own way, however. Perhaps not the best trait to share!

David and Victoria Beckham

Victoria is incredibly hard-working and driven – check out those long and straight lower zones, tall upper zones and rightward slant. She is immensely proud but there is also sign of a temper at times. Look at the small ticks on some of the letters and the defensive, curved-in 'W'.

David matches her willpower (look at the straight and long 't' bars). He can be very down to earth and knows how to defuse any less than chirpy behaviour. The disconnection of some of his letters also shows that he is intuitive and has the ability to second-guess others' needs and wants.

They may have had their ups and downs but this couple have empathy and staying power.

Now have a look at the sample that you and your partner wrote at the beginning of the chapter. Do you still think you and your other half are a good match? Let's hope so!

Chapter 20

CAREER GUIDANCE

The days of needing to know at the age of eighteen exactly how the next fifty years will pan out professionally are thankfully long over, with many of us expecting to have several different jobs throughout our working life.

But for many of us that flexibility actually makes decision-making harder. At the same time we can feel lost when we leave school or university with qualifications that don't actually lead us down an obvious career path.

This can also apply when you've been working for many years, you fancy a complete change, and you don't know what you're looking for. Are you a self-starter? Or an entrepreneurial type who is prepared to take risks? Or do you feel much more comfortable in a salaried position working as part of a team? But what sort of a team? Are you creative? Great with detail? Or perhaps you are drawn to a job in the construction industry? Do you prefer working outside? Working with animals?

Psychometric testing and other tools used by career guidance professionals can be extremely useful for highlighting the areas where your talents lie. Traits can be assessed based on multiple-choice questions to gauge character-istics such as:

Self-confidence.
Creativity.
Leadership qualities.

Logic vs intuition.
Adaptability.
Ability to be a team player.
Social attitude.

The problem with multiple-choice questions and answers is the implication that everyone is meant to fit into a preordained category or box. Why should we? Our personality and our skills are unique, and graphology can help us identify these.

Examining our handwriting can help us to confirm or disagree with what we already think about ourselves.

I cannot possibly list all the millions of different jobs and opportunities out there, but here are a few sectors that require a variety of different skills. Career guidance is far from an exact science, but to help you further I have listed some personality traits and their handwriting counterparts that could be useful in these different careers.

Perhaps at the end of this chapter you may decide that it is time to make that career move you've always been dreaming of . . .

SALES

I think you'll look great in this!

It doesn't matter if you're selling tacks or trucks, certain personality traits are going to be more successful than others in sales, and if you don't possess any of these then you may be in the wrong job.

Enthusiasm and vitality
Slight right slant, good pressure, large size, connected letters, strong 't' bars.

Self-confidence
Large middle zone, even spacing, large ovals, some embellishment allowed. Large personal pronoun.

Resilience
Firm pressure, end strokes (not too long), upward slant.

Gift of the gab
Some open ovals, garlanded connection strokes.

Quick thinking
Good form quality, absence of start strokes.

Intuition
Some disconnected letters.

Persuasion
Some angled connection.

FINANCE

I've got it all figured

To be an accountant or financial director, you'll need a head for figures.

Good with detail
Small size, regularity of size and spacing, high form quality, carefully placed 't' bars and 'i' dots.

Integrity

High form quality, closed ovals, absence of embellishment.

Good organisational skills

Absence of tangling, balanced zones, balanced spacing.

THE CREATIVE ARTS

Beautiful work

This is a huge area and can range from potter to painter, writer to actor. However, without some shared characteristics it may be that you missed your vocation as a bank clerk . . .

Unusual creativity

Interesting letter strokes, large size, tall upper zone and/or long lower zone, firm pressure.

Ability to work alone

Large spaces between words.

Intuition

Disconnection between letters.

Imagination

Tall upper zone.

Sensuality

Long lower zone, shaded ovals, heavy pressure.

Artistic temperament

Heavy pressure, uneven letter sizes, some angular strokes.

MANUAL WORK/CONSTRUCTION

Great manual dexterity

Some of us prefer to work with our hands rather than being stuck behind a desk all day. Do you have the strength?

Manual dexterity
Firm pressure, connected letters, flattened top to 'm' and 'n' letters.

Practicality
Large middle zone, joined-up letters.

Good energy levels
Healthy pressure (not too strong), long lower zone.

Pride in one's work
Long 't' bars, even zones, good form quality.

MEDICINE

how are you feeling?

As well as lots of relevant science qualifications and talent, you should also possess . . .

Empathy
Garland connection strokes, small middle zone.

Ability to handle detail
Small size, even spacing and pressure.

Excellent judgement
Tall upper zone, even spacing and size.

Good energy
Firm pressure, long lower zone.

Analytical mind
Connected letters, angle connection.

Integrity
Closed ovals.

Patience
Garlanded starting strokes, absence of ticks and explosive ovals.

PUBLISHING

Turning over a new leaf.

You'll be bookish, hopefully, but do you have what it takes to bring an idea from conception to the bookshop?

Patience
Garland connections, start and end strokes, even pressure.

Analytical ability
Some angle connections, small middle zone.

Literary ability
Literary 'd' stroke would be helpful!

Verbal skills

Garland connection, small spaces between words, some open ovals.

Good with detail

Small middle zone, carefully placed 't' bars and 'i' dots.

Diplomacy

Closed ovals, garland connection.

POLICE/SECURITY INDUSTRY

Evening all!

This demanding and highly trusted profession requires a lot more than a uniform.

Good judgement

Even zone size, even spacing.

Empathy

Garland connection strokes, small middle zone.

Integrity

Closed ovals.

Open-mindedness

Rightward slant, some loops.

Energy

Good pressure, long lower zone.

Quick reactions

Absence of lead-in strokes.

Intuition
Disconnection of some letters.

Stable emotions
Even size, spacing, pressure; absence of ticks and sharp angles; not too heavy pressure; high form quality.

ENTREPRENEUR

Are you prepared to take a risk for the next deal?

Risk-taking
Not overly rigid regularity, long lower zone.

Strong imagination
Tall upper zone.

Independence
Strong personal pronoun, wide spaces between words, creative letter forms.

Attention to detail
Closed ovals, carefully placed 't' bars and 'i' dots.

Willpower
Long 't' bars, heavy pressure.

HOSPITALITY

You are most welcome

Always fancied owning your own hotel or restaurant?

Leadership qualities
Strong personal pronoun, strong middle zone, no tangling of lines, firm pressure.

Initiative
Large size, firm pressure, absence of start strokes.

People-orientated/sociable
Garland connections, small space between words, large size, open ovals.

Self-discipline
Firm pressure, regularity of size, spacing and pressure.

Attention to detail
Carefully placed 't' bars and 'i' dots, even spacing.

Even temperament
Slight right slant, even pressure, absence of ticks and angles, garland connection strokes.

LEGAL PROFESSION

In the doch...

Think yourself a good 'judge' of character?

Leadership ability
Strong personal pronoun, tall upper zone, good form quality.

Integrity
Closed ovals, high form quality, balanced zones.

Writing ability
Tall upper zone, even middle-zone letters, high form quality.

Strong intellect
Tall upper zone, high form quality, fast speed without compromising on accuracy.

Stable emotions
Even size, spacing, pressure; absence of ticks and sharp angles; not too heavy pressure; high form quality.

Verbal ability
Some open ovals, garland connection strokes.

JOURNALIST/MEDIA

Stop the press...

You may have the scoop, but do you have the scope of qualities needed?

Versatility
Mixed lower-zone shapes, rightward slant, absence of rigid strokes.

Writing talent
High form quality, tall upper zone, fast speed.

Independence
Strong personal pronoun, disconnected letters, high form quality.

Charm
Some open ovals, garland connection strokes, small spaces between words.

Good with detail
Closed ovals, accurately placed 'i' dots and 't' bars, even spacing.

Forward thinking
Rightward slant, small right margin, fast speed.

SOCIAL WORKER

Let me help you.

Do you naturally want to help others?

Empathy
Rightward slant, even zone size, even pressure, garland connection strokes.

Tact and diplomacy
Closed ovals, regularity of spacing and size, straight baseline.

Excellent organisational skills
Regularity of spacing, size and pressure; small middle zone; no tangling.

Patience
Legibility, average speed, closed ovals, even pressure (not heavy).

REAL ESTATE/PROPERTY

Step right inside.

Love 'em or hate 'em – we need 'em . . .

Good with the general public
Connected letters, garland strokes, medium to large size, some open ovals.

Enthusiasm
Large size, long lower zone, rising baseline.

Good with detail
Small size, carefully placed 'i' dots and 't' bars.

Gift of the gab/negotiation skills
Some open ovals, large size, no tangling of lines, firm pressure.

SELF-EMPLOYED

I can get it done.

It doesn't matter what your business is, but if you want to work for yourself then you need very particular skills.

Independence
Wide spaces between words, strong personal pronoun, wide spaces between lines, tall upper zone.

Willpower
Medium to strong pressure, medium to large middle zone, long 't' bars.

Good physical energy
Long lower zone, medium to heavy pressure, regularity of size, spacing, etc.

Diplomacy
Closed ovals, even spacing, even pressure.

Excellent organisational skills
High form quality, small size, regular spacing, legibility, upright slant.

GRAPHOLOGIST

Thats one obviously!

Last but absolutely not least . . .

Analytical ability
Connected letters, angled formations and connection strokes, small middle zone.

Intuition
Disconnected letters, thread formation, tall upper zone.

Tact
Closed ovals, small size, even spacing and pressure.

Determination
Rightward slant, firm pressure, strong 't' bars.

Communication skills
Connected letters, garland strokes, end strokes.

Ability to work on one's own
Medium to large spaces between words, regular spacing, medium to heavy pressure.

You may be rather confused, as a great deal of the individual characteristics for each profession appear to be contradictory and even appear to negate each other. The fact is that there are many, many qualities that are desirable for each profession but none are hard and fast. Just a few from the list would mean that you are probably on the right track. In the same way that matchmaking is not an exact science, neither is pairing an individual off with their perfect job or career.

What can you deduce from your own handwriting? Do you feel that you are on the right track? If not, then what conclusions do you come to after reading this chapter?

Exercise 21: Career Guidance

Can you tell which of these three writing samples would be best suited to a:

A. Writer

B. Doctor

C. Industrial designer

1   Looking for a job

2   Looking for a job

3   Looking for a job

1. This writer shows creativity, constructive ability, energy – I would say that industrial design is the perfect fit for this candidate.

2. Independence, good imagination, intuition – write on.

3. Attention to detail, good communicator, logical – medicine could be prescribed for this candidate.

Can you work out the professions of the following eminent characters?

These three men are all called Charles but they had very different roles in life . . .

Charles De Gaulle

Charles Laughton

Charles Darwin

Now how about these three Janes . . .

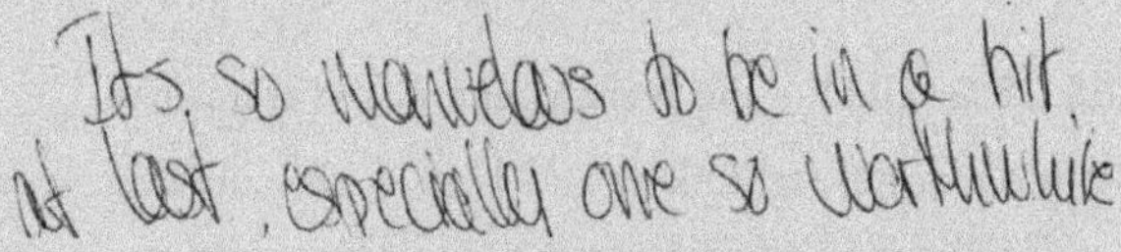
It's so marvelous to be in a hit at last, especially one so worthwhile

Jane Fonda

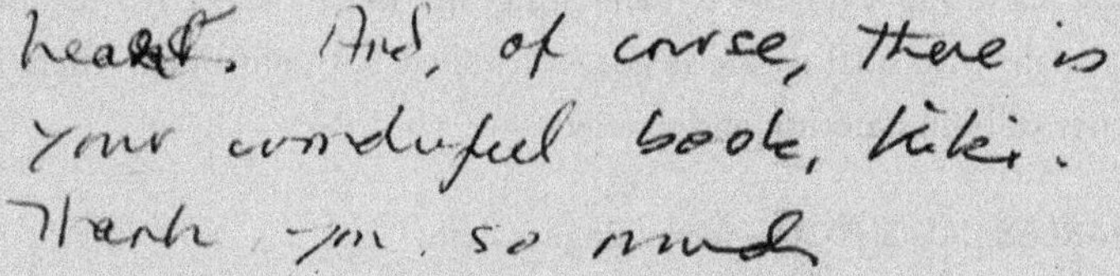
heart. And, of course, there is your wonderful book, Kiki. Thank you so much

Jane Goodall

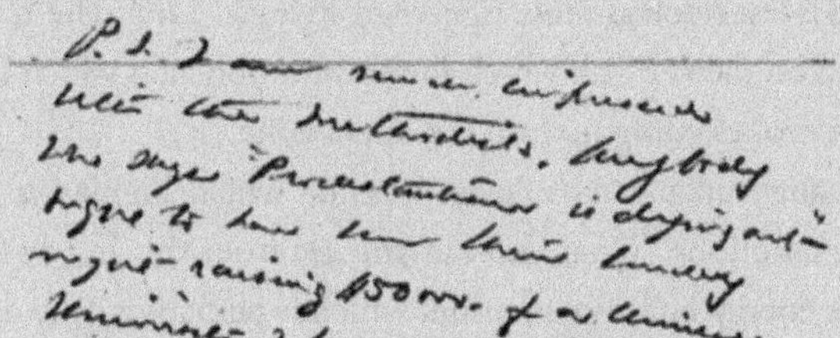
April 30 – 1901

Jane Addams

This was a tough quiz. Let's see how you did – don't despair if you weren't able to match the handwriting to the profession, as all six writers have various qualities which would have allowed them to go into very different careers.

It is up to you to say whether you think they are or were suited to their professions.

Answers

A. CHARLES DE GAULLE – the French general and statesman

The small middle zone, right slant and large spaces between words show a man who is intelligent and independent, but prepared to listen to others despite a natural inclination for being rather shy.

There is a strong regularity to the writing, although it is speedy and efficient with a high form quality. He is goal-orientated but controlled. There is an efficiency of both emotion and energy.

B. CHARLES LAUGHTON – iconic English actor

This Charles shows huge creativity and enormous emotion with a large-sized handwriting, balloon-like lower zone, heavy pressure and filled-in ovals.

The speed is fast (look at those rightward-flying 't' bars). The 't' bars are also highly placed on the vertical, which shows ambition, and which is backed up by the angle strokes going up into the upper zone.

Charles Laughton has an uneven baseline which highlights a man that relies on his emotions. What else can you see from this handwriting? I can detect excess energy but also emotion, which is perhaps a little darker, and a little more repressed. What do you make of his personal pronoun?

C. CHARLES DARWIN – naturalist

Charles Darwin shows many of the characteristics of a scientist. The middle zone is angled and small, the spaces between the words large, but the letters themselves are narrow.

He was very much an intellectual, with reason overruling emotion, but he was also an excellent observer. His thinking is analytical and critical, but if you look at the flying and extremely long 't' bars, there is also evidence of determination and self-protection.

D. JANE FONDA – American actress, writer, political activist and fitness guru

The overall size is large, especially in the middle zone, which would imply that Jane Fonda shares the same trait as many performers and enjoys being in the public eye. There is certainly a healthy ego, but there is also a left slant and very narrow letters with narrow spacing between letters and words.

Despite her need for company there is also much introspection, and the looped and knotted ovals (look at the letter 'a') also point to secrecy and a desire to keep her private life private.

E. JANE GOODALL – scientist and conservationist

This handwriting is somewhat irregular but simplified and with a fast speed. She shows both arcaded and thread connecting strokes.

Jane Goodall is intelligent, with an original and speedy mind. She is capable of calling a spade a spade (unlikely to put up with any monkey business) but she is also thoughtful and considerate to others. There is some falling off at the end of the lines – this is likely to be a result of tiredness.

F. JANE ADDAMS – American social worker, philosopher and suffragette

This Jane's handwriting is hard to read, to say the least, so we could say that it is fairly illegible, but with a fast and fluid hand. Most of the strokes are angled or thread and she has a mixture of lower-zone formations.

Another fast thinker, she shows impatience and versatility in her handwriting. Perhaps surprisingly the heavy pressure and filled-in ovals also show sensuality.

The right slant is strong and the spaces between the words are quite small. She reaches out to others and shows a natural inclination to be empathetic.

As you can see, career guidance, placement or counselling can be a tricky business, and we don't always utilise all the skills that we have, but with enough adaptability and energy we can always change career!

CONCLUSION

I hope you feel confident now that you can apply your new-found knowledge by practising on friends and family. You have a fun and valuable skill to help you understand the people in your life a little better.

I particularly hope you've discovered how significant this multilayered skill is that we all have literally at the end of our fingertips. During my career as a graphologist, I have lost count of how many times I have been told that 'nobody handwrites anything any more'. It is difficult to contend that handwriting is alive and well when there are so many modern forms of communication from WhatsApp to Twitter.

However, the term 'social media' says it all. Don't we all still appreciate a more intimate and personal form of communication, or have we become emotionally disempowered by our use of email and text?

Of course in the same way that a painted portrait was the only way to record a likeness of an individual before the advent of photography, so handwriting used to be the only way to record a communication. Certainly, before finger printing and DNA analysis, handwriting may have been a relevant item in a crime scene.

Handwriting will never go away. The fact is, we are still taught to write at school because we are the only species on the planet that can communicate our feelings with writing and symbols.

Learning to write helps children to develop fine motor control and helps to preserve our memory as we grow older (it is a fact that writing something down helps to embed the thought or fact in our mind).

It is also, as this book has shown, a unique form of identification! Handwriting really is supremely individualistic, creative and as unique as our fingerprints, our DNA and our Facebook profile. Which is why so many people still find it very valuable. From the financial institution S. G. Warburg, which has used graphology to analyse prospective candidates, to Sir Richard Branson, who employed graphologists as an alternative mile-high entertainment for his 'upper-class' passengers, it still fascinates.

Without handwriting, our ability to judge ourselves and others, our innate intuition, will decline.

It is hardly surprising that if we don't communicate by observing the faces of those we are communicating with, or even looking at the road ahead, and instead rely on a tablet or screen for information, then we are in danger of being duped.

Thousands of years ago, our forebears learned to smell danger and sense the enemy. Psychologists later found formulas to help us assess people through body language, linguistic patterns and so on. All of these skills demand eyes and ears to be used in proximity to real people, not screens.

As we become less and less able to use our innate human skills to analyse people, we become more and more vulnerable to extortion, cybercrime and large-scale criminal activity.

We need to be more in tune with ourselves and others, and use all of our available human skills to dig deeper into our psyche. As we live in a world of fast-moving and competitive social media so we become more obsessed with ourselves and our own worlds, whether that's through the selfie stick, Twitter or Instagram 'likes'. Unfortunately our insecurity grows along with our social media 'friends' and 'followers'.

All forms of psychology are important and will become more and more so in the future as we struggle to understand the real world around us. We know that in moments of disagreement 'the pen is mightier than the sword' but it is also mighty when it comes to graphology. Never has this humble writing instrument felt more relevant.

ACKNOWLEDGEMENTS

I have love and gratitude for everyone who has made my career such enormous fun. It's thanks to you all that I can still be so passionate about graphology and the people that I have met along the journey.

This book has been a joy to write, and I would like to thank my wonderful agent, Jo Unwin, for her foresight, encouragement and belief in me. Thank you also to Jo's fantastic and hard-working team, Milly and Donna. Thanks to Arvon, for introducing me to Jo and kick-starting all sorts of exciting changes in my life.

My heartfelt thanks and affection to my editor, Katy Follain, who has been simply brilliant, as well as to the whole team at Quercus. Thanks, in particular, to Alison MacDonald and Ana McLaughlin for their attention to detail and patience with me.

This book would be nothing without my enormously talented illustrator, Amber Anderson, to whom I am hugely grateful for making the process so easy and fun.

Thanks to David Bache for his contributions – both practical and artistic – and for his welcome guidance. An enormous thank you also must go to my beautiful children, Theo and Clemmie, for their patience, love and technological support – 'Have you tried switching it off and on again?'.

To my friends, who have helped keep me sane, not only during the last year, but always. Without your love, friendship and support through the laughter and the tears, nothing would be possible. I am so lucky to have you all in my life.

A special thanks to my friend, Victoria Keeble, who introduced me to graphology all those years ago and was with me when the story first began.

Last but not least, an enormous thank you to the few dissenters and naysayers in my life who have given me the determination and sheer bloody-mindedness to carry on.